Advance Praise for *Write the Right Words*

"Sandra Lamb's book reinforces the principles of etiquette, reminding us that writing personal notes is a vital way of sharing appreciation and respect with others. Handwritten correspondence is an art form that is far from lost."

—Peggy Post, etiquette expert and author

"Sandra Lamb gently reminds us that the tried-and-true values of the past are still part of connecting to others in the present. In helping us find the words, she gives us a gift we can pass along to our children." —Andrea Warren, author of *Orphan Train Rider: One Boy's True Story*

"Lamb reminds us of the value of personal connections and etiquette in all our relationships." —Mary Mihaly, author of *The 250 Questions Every Self-Employed Person Should Ask*

"If you've ever sat down to write a note of condolence, congratulations, announce good or bad news, or any other personal or business note and found yourself at a loss for words, this book is for you. . . . Wherever you write, at home or at the office, your writing equipment should include a copy of this book. You'll find yourself turning to it again and again." —Tina B. Tessina, Ph.D., author, blogger, and professional counselor

Also by SANDRA E. LAMB

Personal Notes

How to Write It

Write the

THE

RIGHT WORDS

MESSAGES FROM THE

HEART FOR

EVERY OCCASION

SANDRA E. LAMB

ST. MARTIN'S PRESS

NEW YORK

For Charles

www.stmartins.com

Library of Congress Cataloging-in-Publication Data

Lamb, Sandra E.
    Write the right words : messages from the heart for every occasion / Sandra E.
Lamb.—1st ed.
        p. cm.
    ISBN 978-0-312-59627-9
    1. Letter writing.   2. Interpersonal relations.   3. English language—
Rhetoric.   I. Title.
    PE1483.L38 2010
    808.6—dc22   2009047579

First Edition: May 2010

10   9   8   7   6   5   4   3   2

CONTENTS

Introduction   ix

A Time-Honored Tradition   x

You, the Sender   x

Writing Out Your Feelings   xi

Writing Is Connecting   xii

PART ONE: CONNECTING MESSAGES

The Art of Connecting with Greeting Cards   3

Ready, Set, Send   4

PART TWO: HAPPY DAY MESSAGES

Make It a Celebration   9

Birthday   11

Graduation   19

Engagement   29

Wedding   33

Anniversary   40

Births and Adoptions   48

Congratulations   55
Rites of Passage and Life Events   60
Welcome   66
New Home   70

PART THREE: HOLIDAY MESSAGES

New Year's Day   77
Valentine's Day   80
St. Patrick's Day   83
Easter   85
May Day and Spring   87
Mother's Day   90
Father's Day   97
Independence Day   103
Rosh Hashanah (The Jewish New Year)   105
Christmas   108
Hanukkah (The Jewish Festival of Lights)   113
Kwanzaa   116

PART FOUR: SOCIAL GRACE MESSAGES

Thank You   123
Appreciation   129
Bon Voyage   134
Retirement   136
Friendship and Family   140
Just a Note; Thinking About You; To Cheer You   146
Love Notes (and Letters)   150

PART FIVE: CARE AND CONCERN MESSAGES

Get Well   159
Loss   172

PART SIX: CREATING A NEW RELATIONSHIP
   MESSAGES
Family Members   207
Restoring a Relationship   216

PART SEVEN: DATES TO REMEMBER
January   229
February   230
March   231
April   232
May   233
June   234
July   235
August   236
September   237
October   238
November   239
December   240

INTRODUCTION

There's a very special feeling you get—all hugged and warm—when you open your mailbox and find a hand-addressed envelope. There it is, with your name written in the penmanship of someone special to you.

Maybe it's a birthday card from a dear aunt, or one from a close friend. She didn't forget. You are remembered. Anticipating the message inside makes you feel connected to the sender even before you tear the envelope open; connected in a way you wouldn't have felt if your aunt or friend had just sent an email—even an animated one containing a chorus of dancing emoticons—or, if she had rung you up on the telephone (though that would have been a special brand of *nice* all its own!).

There just is no substitute for a personal greeting card with a handwritten message. It can be saved, and read again and again. It contains something of the personality of the sender. Something both the sender and "sendee" will cherish. Something that connects them together in a very special way.

But the real test comes, of course, after the envelope has been opened. Even the birthday card with a beautifully expressed verse will leave you, the birthday girl, feeling let down if there's no personal, handwritten message from Auntie. It's that heart-felt, handwritten message in her own personal pen that makes you feel really connected to her. You know she cares. You know she has invested something of herself. You feel the length and breadth of her love in the familiar curve of her handwriting.

A Time-Honored Tradition

The first greeting card may have been an Egyptian papyrus scroll, or a display of artistically arranged Chinese characters that conveyed a message of goodwill for the New Year. As early as the 1400s in Europe, handcrafted greeting cards made of paper were being delivered from one person to another to express personal greetings. The practice grew over the centuries, and was trans-formed to general popularity with the advent of the printing press. Then the method of delivery was speeded up and made more affordable with the introduction of the postage stamp on May 1, 1840, in Great Britain and Ireland. The first postage stamps in the United States, bearing the images of George Washington and Benjamin Franklin, were introduced in 1847.

You, the Sender

The challenge comes when you are the sender. How do you write a greeting-card message to someone that will infuse your words with that special bit of care? With your own voice? With a hug that's warm and beating and alive? How do you write a message that pulses with a visceral thread of connection?

We all sometimes feel message-challenged. And, of course, you want to make your message fresh and personal. Heartfelt. You may even want to make your message funny or clever.

Writing Out Your Feelings

There's ample anecdotal evidence that the act of writing by hand—if engaged in, systematically and routinely, over a period of time—will take you to a deeper level of *yourself.* It's been successfully used in psychoanalysis, in correctional institutions, and in creative development programs.

Try this. Sit down with several blank sheets of paper, pose a question to yourself from your experience—maybe something like, "I felt _____ when _____ happened." Fill in the words, and make them specific. Better yet, fill in the blanks with an experience you've wanted to better understand.

After you've formed your question, and without lifting your pen tip from the paper, write on this topic for five minutes straight without stopping. Time yourself.

After you're finished, check yourself. What do you feel? What have you experienced? Have you realized a transitioning from the level of complete awareness of yourself sitting in your chair, to the level of thinking about the question, to the deeper level of feeling those emotions within the memories you've expressed? Did you feel the creative juices of expression while writing them out?

What about discovery? Did you discover something about your emotions during that original experience as you reprocessed it that you hadn't really thought about or processed before this exercise? Is there a certain sense of accomplishment, a sense of having created something, or having discovered something you had not yet discovered during this act of writing?

Joan Didion, in an interview with Charlie Rose, said of writing her book *The Year of Magical Thinking,* which chronicled the year after the sudden death of her husband, John Gregory Dunne, "I have to write things down to know what I'm thinking . . ." And then, "What helped me to survive was writing this book . . ." Most people in my classes, where I've employed this technique of self-discovery through writing, have been quite amazed about where the writing experience took them, and what they took away from it.

Social scientists are timid about making the correlation between mental health and the act of writing by hand, but there have been studies that do link the ability to read and spell in early childhood with the act of writing by hand. And there has been voiced concern from many quarters that the latest computer-native generation not only will be unable to write legibly, but they may also be missing some very essential mental and emotional developmental building blocks, as well.

Additionally, the therapeutic use of handwriting in the treatment of neuroses, and even some psychoses, has a long and well-documented history as a very useful tool in realizing healing.

Writing Is Connecting

So, in truth, your handwritten message may be even more beneficial than the joy, support, and comfort you are able to give to the one whose name appears on the outside of the envelope in the addressed-to area. It may be that in the act of handwriting your message, you are also, and first, connecting to your deeper, inner, and better self.

This small volume was created to remind you that there is real value in the handwritten message. It is precious, and it is something we don't want to disappear from our social discourse. Handwritten messages have always been one of the better aspects of civil society. Let's not lose them.

Whatever your objective, this guide will help get you started. It will help you write the card that's the perfect fit: the warm, personal message, which is the heart of even the best-versed and most beautiful greeting card; the funniest quips; the sympathetic and empathetic words that provide comfort in a very dark hour.

Use this guide as your own private message-flow-starter. And, oh yes, each chapter contains "Quotable Quotes," which are included first for your own inspiration for writing. Sometimes, you may want to simply use a quote in your message with credit to the original author to add weight, depth, and flair to your own message.

The life which is not examined is not worth living.
—*Plato,* Greek philosopher

The power of the word is real whether or not
you are conscious of it.
Your own words are the bricks and mortar of the
dreams you want to realize.
Behind every word flows energy.
—*Sonia Choquette,* American author and teacher

When we create something, we always create it first
in a thought form.
—*Shakti Gawain,* American author and teacher

It is only with the heart that one can see rightly;
what is essential is invisible to the eye.
—*Antoine De Saint-Exupéry,* French aviator and writer

Like an ability or a muscle, hearing your inner wisdom
is strengthened by doing it.
—*Robbie Gass,* American musician

Get in touch with the silence within yourself and know
that everything in this life has a purpose.
—*Elisabeth Kübler-Ross,* American scientist and author

I shall become a master in this art only after a
great deal of practice.
—*Erich Fromm,* German psychoanalyst and social theorist

Do not hurry; do not rest.
—*Johann Wolfgang Von Goethe,* German poet, playwright, and author

The words that enlighten the soul are more
precious than jewels.
—*Hazrat Inayat Khan,* Indian musician, poet, and spiritual leader

Not the why, but the what.
—*Ernest Hemingway,* American author

The messages within these pages will offer a new perspective, save you lots of time, and help you break through your writer's block.

Sometimes you may decide to use the message exactly as it appears on these pages, but usually you'll want to adapt the message slightly to fit your personality and what you're feeling at the moment.

PART ONE

Connecting Messages

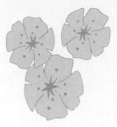

The Art of Connecting with Greeting Cards

In order to draw a connecting line from your heart to the heart of the person to whom you're sending a greeting card with your handwritten message, you'll want to infuse the card with light and life, hope and spirit. Your handwritten message supplies what's so often missing in our lives: the richness of shared humanity, and the sense that we are connected one to another.

Focus

To get your creative juices flowing quickly and easily, focus your thoughts on the person to whom you're writing, turn to the related section in this little volume, and then review the created notes to rev up your creative engine.

List

You may want to start by listing—on a piece of scratch paper—the top three attributes you love and admire about the person. Is she brave, thoughtful, original, funny, determined, loyal, creative, or admirably unique?

Remember

Now, think of a memory you have of her exhibiting that very special character attribute you've chosen. You may want to state the attribute and then use a very short anecdote to underscore your point: "You are one of the bravest people I know. Your volunteer work in the VA Hospital this year demonstrated the courage of heart that's yours. What a very special person you are."

In addition, you may want to reinforce the message in the greeting card by underscoring a key word or two in the card's message, and then add a few lines of your own: "It's true, Susan. You possess creativity in spades. Who else could have come up with the terrific interactive Website you designed? No one!"

It can be as simple as that. But it's always going to be your special handwritten message that is going to carry the water. The very best and most beautiful prepared greeting-card message won't get indelibly connected to you, and you to the recipient, unless you connect the dots in a personal way.

Ready, Set, Send

Our foremothers had the right idea in keeping all their writing materials together in a safe and central (perhaps nearly sacred) place: a well-kept, leather-bound book of addresses and dates with notations, a supply of personal cards and stationery, a very special pen or two, and postage stamps. It was all snuggled into a cozy corner in the secretary desk and at-the-ready. Sitting down and writing was a routine thing. Maybe they even considered it a daily activity of leisure. Something to do while having jam and bread and tea in the middle of the afternoon, perhaps?

To put ease, leisure, and enjoyment back into the process for your message writing in our mad, mad world, here are a few simple points to make it all go easier. And faster. We must always have faster, mustn't we?

Decide on a place that makes sense for you to keep and write greeting cards. Maybe you'll want to borrow from Elizabeth Barrett Browning, and put all the necessary things in a laptop desk, or a hardcover box, which you can use held in your lap, while sitting in your favorite lounge chair.

Collect all the memorable dates and occasions, and record them in one book—in the back of this book would be good—arranged by month and day. You'll undoubtedly want to include birthdays, anniversaries, holidays, and special occasions. You'll certainly want to include the special days the recipients celebrate. Be sure to make notations about birth years (especially for children, so you know exactly which birthday age is approaching), wedding anniversary dates, the dates of death, etc., and any special facts that may be important to your messages.

Near the end of each month, check your record and purchase all the greeting cards you'll need for the next month. It'll help if you make this a standard and fun shopping trip when you can be a little relaxed and think about the messages you wish to send.

You may prefer to write a week's, a half month's, or even a whole month's greeting-card messages at one time. Arrange the cards in a storage box (by date), or file, with the date you'll want to put each in the mail in the upper right-hand corner where you'll later place the stamp. Or, write the date on a sticky note you can remove.

Make it a habit to check your cards each week, so you don't let a date slip by.

Note: It's very nice to include some small gift item in the envelope. Children, particularly, will enjoy something enclosed in the card. Colorful stickers are great; so are balloons, or tiny books. A stick or flat container of sugarless gum or a lollipop—if the parents approve—is also a delight to a child. Even a dollar, a pin, or a little "prize," such as a magnifying glass or a backpack bauble, will put a smile on a small face.

For adults, you may want to put in a photo that brings back very happy memories, a bookmark, a gift card, or something creative, like a clipping from the newspaper dated the day of the recipient's birth—if it's her birthday.

At-the-ready in your "writing desk" should be a generous supply of greeting cards and your own personal note cards that you'll use for those "thinking-about-you" notes, and thank-you notes. You'll undoubtedly want to keep a supply of "thinking-about-you" cards, sympathy cards, and get-well cards on hand, too, for sending off at a moment's notice. But never be without your own supply of personal note cards, which you may use for any occasion to carry your message.

PART TWO

Happy Day Messages

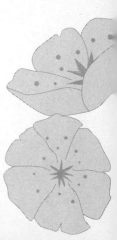

Make It a Celebration

You will add to the beauty of any celebration by sending a greeting card. It helps increase the recipient's joy. You can make your message even more special by including a few words of your admiration for the recipient, or a related memory about her that will bring a smile of recognition and a sense of your shared history that she'll savor. Building these kinds of memories knits a thread of connection between the two of you. Don't miss an opportunity to do it.

Message Etiquette

The only rule here is your desire to add to the joy of another soul on an occasion she regards as noteworthy, to increase her joy. If you check your message against this standard, you won't go astray.

QUOTABLE QUOTES

Remember me when I am gone away,
Gone far away into the silent land.
—*Christina Georgina Rossetti,* English poet

You start by writing to live.
You end by writing so as not to die.
—*Carlos Fuentes,* Mexican author, scholar, and diplomat

The most beautiful things are those
that madness prompts and reason writes.
—*André Gide,* French author and Nobel Prize winner

Thought flies and words go on foot.
Therein lies all the drama of a writer.
—*Julien Green,* French-American author

The secret of all good writing is sound judgment.
—*Horace,* Roman satirist

What is written without effort is in
general read without pleasure.
—*Samuel Johnson,* English author

It is one test of a fully developed writer
that he reminds us of no one but himself.
—*Melvin Maddocks,* American journalist and author

You can stroke people with words.
—*F. Scott Fitzgerald,* American author

Birthday

Think of a birthday as a celebration of the person! It's the perfect opportunity to tell someone how special she is, and to give her your best wishes for a terrific day and a wonderful upcoming year.

The advent of birthday celebrations emerged after there were calendars to mark the year, month, and day. In the early societies in Egypt, China, and Rome, there are records of celebrations of the birthdays of royalty and other important people.

The first printed birthday greeting may date back to as early as fifteenth-century Germany, where greetings on paper were printed from woodcuts.

Surviving greeting cards printed in Germany four centuries ago still look beautiful today. Some from the 1890s depict delicate floral arrangements in shades of pastels, featuring little opening flaps and cutout windows; and some are outfitted with silk ribbon and lace edges. These were obviously created with the Victorian woman in mind.

Today, your personal birthday greeting-card message can take so many forms. The options range from your own written message on your own personal (blank) note card to a commercial greeting card with a printed message, which may now also be equipped to record your own voice message with background music.

Plus, there is always the charming option of creating your own greeting card with photos the recipient will cherish, or your own original art.

Message Etiquette

For *children,* no event could be bigger than a birthday! It's a complete and wonderful celebration totally focused on her; and so should your message be.

Children love silly poems, questions, puzzles, and the anticipation of yet another surprise. You can use all of these wisely in the message you send. Why not include something like a "Love Coupon" or IOU to be redeemed for a special future fun adventure? It could be a trip to the zoo, an ice cream sundae at the ice cream shop, a ball game, or a fishing trip. Also, slipping in a dollar for each year of the child's life, or stamps for her collection, buttons, stickers, balloons, or hair barrettes are good ideas. Even in these days of mega–birthday parties, small envelope gifts are special.

For adults, it's important to know how the person you're writing to feels about her birthday before you begin. If she's sensitive or secretive about her age, for example, don't mention it. Your message should put—and keep—the positive spotlight on the birthday girl. Comments about youself are best given only as validation and to shine the spotlight on the recipient.

Be sure you understand her sense of humor before including a humorous remark. The best rule is to use self-deprecating humor—poking fun at yourself. Still, be sure your message doesn't infer that the statement also applies to the recipient. For example, if you're writing a friend who is celebrating her 50th year, to say "I've discovered that turning 50 means everything begins to sag," could communicate the wrong message, and doesn't meet your objective of contributing to her celebratory mood.

If you want to add a small envelope gift to your adult message, try something like a recipe the birthday girl has envied, "Karen's Macadamia Nut Cookies," written out in your own pen on a recipe card. Or, you might send a special bookmark for the woman you know loves to read, a newspaper clipping from the date she was born, a gift card, a memorable photograph from the near or more distant past, a lottery ticket, or even commemorative postage stamps. A "Love Coupon" that promises you'll perform an act of love that the birthday girl will enjoy, like "Good for One High Tea at My House, Thursday, April 10, 3:00 P.M.," will delight her, too. Be creative.

QUOTABLE QUOTES

It is not the years in your life but
the life in your years that counts.
—*Adlai Stevenson,* American politician and diplomat

Celebrate the happiness that friends are always giving,
make every day a holiday and celebrate just living!
—*Amanda Bradley,* American poet and essayist

The same old charitable lie
Repeated as the years scoot by
Perpetually makes a hit . . .
"You really haven't changed a bit."
—*Margaret Fishback Powers,* American poet and author

I'm tired of all this nonsense about beauty
being only skin-deep. That's deep enough.
What do you want—an adorable pancreas?
—*Jean Kerr,* American author and playwright

Now I am beginning to live a little,
and feel less like a sick oyster at low tide.
—*Louisa May Alcott,* American author

It's the good girls who keep diaries;
the bad girls never have the time.
—*Tallulah Bankhead,* American actor

Life is too short to stuff a mushroom.
—*Shirley Conran,* English author

Nothing is as good as it seems beforehand.
—*George Eliot (Mary Anne Evans),* English author

Suggested Messages

ADULT—GENERAL

- Bushels of best wishes for a wonderful birthday.
- You always leave things better than you found them. Best wishes for this year—you'll transform it into something very special, I know.
- No one deserves a happier day, or a more delightful year. Deep and abiding wishes that both reflect the wonderful person you are!
- Wishes for a truly sensational day, and a stellar year ahead.
- Here's wishing you a year of new beginnings! Knowing you, you'll make the very most of every single day.
- You've earned a very special year. Here's wishing you the very best one yet!
- The world is brighter for having you in it. You light up a very large circle. Wishing you your brightest year ever!

- You have the ability to turn every situation into an opportunity. I can hardly wait to see what you do with this new year.
- Birthdays are for celebrating, and here's hoping you'll carry on the party for the whole year.
- Special people should have special birthdays. But for *very special people,* like you, the sky's the limit. Do have a smashing good time.
- Happy, happy birthday, and best wishes for all you do this year.
- I believe this is the magical year for all your wishes to come true. I'm thinking, of course, of that trip to Paris.
- I'm smiling all the way to the mailbox just thinking about all the great new adventures you'll be taking on this year. And I'm wishing you success beyond your grandest dreams for each and every one of them.
- Here's hoping your birthday is just a tiny bit as wonderful as you are!
- May all the rewards of your labors be realized in this coming year.
- Love, prayers, and best wishes for a wonderful birthday.
- [Name], here's to a day filled with happiness and an entire year of riches to follow.
- You're the greatest—I, along with so many others, get it. Happy birthday.
- What wonderful, fantastic things will you do this year to add to your impressive life list? I know you'll make a huge success of it, whatever it is. But do tell me over lunch next week, will you?
- Here's wishing you a year more wonderful than the last. I can hardly wait to learn what you'll do with it.

- Another year better. Topping your stellar record is going to be a big challenge, but you—of all the people I know—are up to it.
- Here's to a year of fulfilling all those wonderful dreams. May it be your best year yet!
- Best wishes for a year even more terrific than the last. I can't think of anyone who deserves it more.
- I can't think of a person I'd rather wish a spectacular coming year. I'm sure it will be fantastic, because you are.
- You've made this a better world. In this family, we're all celebrating the day you were born. Will you join us for your birthday cake on [day]?
- To the master of multitasking, and making a great success of everything, best wishes for a record-setting year.
- I have a feeling that this is going to go down as your happiest year yet!
- It's going to be really, really hard to top this past year; but I'm sure you're up to it. Best wishes for the happiest of birthdays, and a year filled with all the joy your life can hold. To overflowing!
- The best of all possible days—that's my wish for your birthday.
- You make life a celebration, [Name]; may you have the full fireworks on your birthday, and a five-star year.
- Wishing my very special friend a very special birthday.
- A very, very special birthday wish for a very, very special friend.
- Friends who have birthdays should be treated to one of those double, double banana splits like we used to eat in high school. How about letting me treat on Friday at Vic's?

- The years have not changed you at all. You're still a very unique brand of "Very Special Woman." So, your birthday will always remain at the top of my list of happy events. This year it's extra special.
- No one deserves it more; no one wears it better—Happy Birthday, [Name].
- May you experience just a small sampling of the happiness you've brought to others, on your day.
- You're wonderful! Happy Birthday.

ADULT—HUMOROUS

- If birthdays were given out by popular demand, you'd be celebrating every week. And you'd always get my vote for best birthday girl!
- Three words to the wise birthday boy: party, party, party. Happy Birthday, [Name].
- I'm switching to the leap-year or dog-year birthday celebration plan. If you weren't such a young pup, I might suggest it for you, too. Have a howling good time on your birthday, you young, sweet thing.
- You always swing for the fences. Best wishes for a real record home-run season this year.
- Did I hear something about boogying all night? You get on down, Girlfriend. You've really got the moves to make it spectacular!
- Remember our sock hops in the gym at noon when we'd try to act two years older? You were so successful at that. And now you are so successful at looking ten years younger. What a woman! Have a great 39th. Again.
- Who knew you were turning one year older? No one would even guess!

- No one really believes that you get *better*, not older. But in your case it's true.

ADULT—RELATIVE

- It was a happy day, indeed, on [date], when you came into this family. And each year we're delighted to celebrate with you the wonderful person you are. We all love you, and are delighted to call you our own!
- You and I share everything—including this date for our birthday. You make me feel very sorry for everyone who doesn't have you as a twin sister. You are the ying to my yang; and the zing in my heart. I love you, Sis. Happy birthday!
- Happy birthday, best sister, best friend.

CHILDREN

- A little butterfly just flew by to remind me that a very, very special little girl named [Name] is having a birthday today!!! I'm singing the birthday song for you. I can hardly wait to hear all the special things you'll do on your very special day.
- What did I hear? Our very big girl is [age] years old? Can it be? Wow, I think that means you'll be able to play soccer on the big girls' team, right?
- Roses are red,
  Violets are blue,
  Someone very special is having a birthday—
  And that someone is YOU!
  Happy, happy, happy birthday, [Name].
- For a girl who's [age] I'm including a special IOU for your mommy to read to you. What do you think it says?

Well, on second thought, a girl who's [age] is also big enough for another IOU, so I've included that one, too. Happy birthday.

- These special stamps are for your collection. I'm betting that you'll finish the whole book this year, now that you're [age]. Happy birthday, [Name].

- I met a little mouse at the animal fair, and he said he needed to tell me a very important secret. What do you think he whispered in my ear? You're right. He said, "Don't forget that today is [Name]'s birthday and she is [age]. Happy, happy birthday. Thank you, Little Birthday Mouse.

- Once upon a time in the land of [Town or State] lived a very special little girl, whose name was [Name]. She was waiting and waiting and waiting for her birthday, so she could turn [age]. And now it's here! HAPPY BIRTHDAY!

Graduation

This is the perfect opportunity to help someone celebrate her accomplishments, and her new opportunities. Applaud and focus on her hard work and achievements.

The historical roots of ceremonies that recognize having mastered a set of skills and the trappings we use in these celebrations—gowns, caps (mortarboards), valedictorian speeches, the playing of "Pomp and Circumstance," the delivery of a sermon and a prayer—began, interestingly enough, very early in Celtic society with the Celtic priests, or Druids. Over the centuries, elements were added by many cultures, weaving into the tapestry of the graduation ceremony nuances of meaning. For example, the colors now used to define different areas of study were probably adopted from the European tradesmen guilds of the Middle Ages. These craft masters distinguished themselves by colors and types and details of their garments. The mortarboard or present-day cap worn for graduation may have originated as a symbol of the bricklaying trade of that same time period.

Oxford University is often credited with formalizing the giving of the baccalaureate degree mid fifteenth century. The march music, "Pomp and Circumstance," written by Sir Edward Elgar, was first played in Liverpool, England, in 1901.

High schools, universities, and many other institutions of higher learning have added their own traditions and special attire to the graduation ceremonies. The different branches of the U.S. armed forces, for example, have their own sets of graduation traditions, which are observed down to the minute detail. Studying all of these may give you some great clues to writing an appropriate message to the graduate, as well as a very unique one.

Message Etiquette

To strike the right note in your message, tune in to the graduate's personal experience and her view of this event. For her, it may be the end of her academic career, or, it may be just a prerequisite step before she gets started on what she considers her real education. Remember, success can only be measured individually. Spin the positive details of who she is and what she has accomplished to add your voice to her celebration. If success was made by the narrowest of margins, emphasize the fact that this is an important milestone, required a great effort, and reflects real accomplishment. If the graduation was made with honors, praise the recipient for an outstanding job. Use specific details of her accomplishments to help make this a very special occasion of celebration.

QUOTABLE QUOTES

I have taken all knowledge to be my province.
—*Francis Bacon,* English scientist and Viscount St. Albans

A mind content both crown and kingdom is.
—*Robert Greene,* American author

Education is what survives when what
has been learned has been forgotten.
—*B. F. Skinner,* American psychologist and author

You cannot help but learn more as you take the world
into your hands. Take it up reverently, for it is an old
piece of clay, with millions of thumbprints on it.
—*John Updike,* American author

Wherever you go, go with all your heart.
—*Confucius,* Chinese philosopher

The heights by great men reached and kept
Were not attained by sudden flight,
But they, while their companions slept,
Were toiling upward in the night.
—*Henry Wadsworth Longfellow,* American poet

Life is my college. May I graduate well,
and earn some honors.
—*Louisa May Alcott,* American author

It is the mark of an educated mind to be able
to entertain a thought without accepting it.
—*Aristotle,* Greek philosopher and educator

It is the object of learning, not only to satisfy the
curiosity and perfect the spirits of ordinary men,
but also to advance civilization.
—*Woodrow Wilson,* American president

Employ thy time well, if thou meanest to get leisure.
—*Benjamin Franklin,* American statesman and philosopher

Victory belongs to the most persevering.
—*Napoléon Bonaparte,* French military and political leader

The things that will destroy America are prosperity
at any price, peace at any price, safety first
instead of duty first, the love of soft living, and
the get-rich-quick theory of life.
—*Theodore Roosevelt,* American president

I do the very best I know how—the very best I can;
and I mean to keep on doing so until the end.
—*Abraham Lincoln,* American president

What lies behind us and what lies before us are tiny
matters compared to what lies within us.
—*Ralph Waldo Emerson,* American essayist and poet

There are no secrets to success. It is the result of
preparation, hard work, and learning from failure.
—*Colin Powell,* American statesman and four-star general

Our best chance for happiness is education.
—*Mark Van Doren,* American teacher and poet

Nothing in the world can take the place of persistence.
—*Calvin Coolidge,* American president

Look up and not down; look out and not in; look
forward and not back; and lend a hand.
—*Edward Everett Hale,* American social reformer and author

There are two educations. One should teach us how to
make a living and the other how to live.
—*John Adams,* American president

Be the change you want to see in the world.
—*Mahatma Gandhi,* Indian spiritual and political leader

Taste the joy that springs from labor.
—*Henry Wadsworth Longfellow,* American poet

Always tell the truth—it's the easiest thing to remember.
—*David Mamet,* American playwright and filmmaker

He that can have patience can have what he will.
—*Benjamin Franklin,* American statesman and philosopher

We gain the strength of the temptation we resist.
—*Ralph Waldo Emerson,* American essayist and poet

The world hates change, yet it is the only
thing that has brought progress.
—*Charles F. Kettering,* American inventor

Experience is not what happens to you;
it is what you do with what happens to you.
—*Aldous Huxley,* English editor, author, and poet

It is better to be faithful than famous.
—*Theodore Roosevelt,* American president

A man who qualifies himself well for his
calling never fails of employment . . .
—*Thomas Jefferson,* American president

If any man seeks for greatness, let him forget
greatness and ask for truth, and he will find both.
—*Horace Mann,* American educator and author

The best things in life aren't things.
—*Art Buchwald,* American humorist and author

Don't ask yourself what the world needs, ask yourself what
makes you come alive. And then go and do that. Because
what the world needs is people who have come alive.
—*Howard Thurman,* American philosopher and author

Human progress has often depended on the courage
of a man who dared to be different.
—*Herbert Prochnow,* American banker and author

The purpose of learning is growth, and our minds, unlike
our bodies, can continue growing as we continue to live.
—*Mortimer Adler,* American philosopher and author

The highest reward for a man's toil is not what he
gets for it, but what he becomes by it.
—*John Ruskin,* English author and art critic

One machine can do the work of fifty ordinary men.
No machine can do the work of one extraordinary man.
—*Elbert Hubbard,* American philosopher and author

Training is everything. The . . . cauliflower is nothing
but cabbage with a college education.
—*Mark Twain,* American humorist and author

Suggested Messages

ADULT

- [Name], you've mastered the formula—work very hard, and take one small step at a time. Congratulations!
- Now you're really ready to take on the world. How far you've come; what a lot you've achieved. Congratulations.
- My hat's off to you, [Name].
- Get ready, world, here comes [Name]! There'll be some changes!

- [Name], you've proven yourself in the most difficult arena; I'm sure great things are in store for you.
- What a marvelous job you've done, [Name]. I hope you are just half as proud of your accomplishments as we are of you. Congratulations.
- Remember when you said you'd never make it to this day? You made it, Champ. Terrific stuff you're made of.
- Next stop, your very own wonderful life.
- You've always reached for the stars. Your hard-won diploma will just help you tip one out of the sky so you can firmly grasp it!
- Congratulations on hanging in there and getting the job done.
- [Name], we know by the way you took on high school— especially that chemistry course last year—that this graduation is just the first in a long string of successes that will be yours.
- What wonderful news, Graduate! Best wishes for that shining career we know you'll have.
- All things come to those who work very hard. I can hardly wait to hear about the things you do, [Name], with your brand-new diploma.
- Whatever you decide to pursue, you've already proven you'll do it very well.
- You have real star status in this household. Congratulations, [Name], on your great accomplishment. It's just the first of many, many, many more.
- So far, you've realized your own dreams through perseverance and self-discipline. All your dreams are within your reach. Congratulations.

- What a bright future you've created for yourself, [Name].
- What a superb job you've done.
- Your five-star efforts have created a record to be very proud of. We're all very proud of you, too.
- Yes, dreams do come true; it has happened to you. We celebrate your success with you. And we look forward to all those future accomplishments that will be yours.
- Once upon a time there was a small boy who didn't want to go to kindergarten. Oh my, look at you now!
- To set your sights on something so difficult, and then to achieve it! We all salute you.
- When you wish upon a star, shoot for the moon, and apply your own particular brand of genius, great things happen. They did. And will continue to in all you do, [Name]. Way to go!
- Many, many people care about you. I'm standing squarely in the front row of your admirers. We're all standing up and applauding you. And we're going to be right here, waiting to hear all about your next great success!
- Genius has its rewards. We know this is only the first, and that there are many, many, many more acts to come. You're terrific, [Name].

CHILD

- A-tisket, a-tasket, now you've got a kindergarten graduation in your basket. What a big boy you are.
- It's up, up, up, and on to first grade now, our kindergarten graduate.
- Wow! A middle-school grad. Awesome!
- It wasn't easy, but you did it, [Name].

- This calls for a celebration. Pizza Night will be Saturday!
- You got through math, and you finished that extracurricular science project. Nothing can stop you now. Way to go!
- We are very, very, very proud of you, [Name].

HUMOR

- You've just blown all the stars right off your chart! Fantastic!
- You made it, even though the dog did eat most of your homework!
- Twinkle, twinkle. You're our star, [Name].
- Over the moon, that's you, [Name]. Way to go.
- Once I wished upon a star. And now that very Star you are. Fantastic!
- Here's to the kid who is different.
  Here's to the kid with an unusual streak.
  And when you are grown, [Name],
  Your achievements will have shown,
  You'll be cleverly and amazingly unique!
  You're just what the whole world needs and is waiting for!
- To the boy who's always as curious as George, put on that yellow hat and get out there!

Engagement

ANNOUNCING AN ENGAGEMENT

A couple who decides to become engaged usually announces the happy news first to family and close friends, then to a wider circle of colleagues and acquaintances. Such good news is best communicated in person, or at least over the telephone. But in this cyber age, announcements to a broader audience may even be done electronically, by email, or maybe a Website will be created for the pair.

Still, make room for a traditional, handwritten announcement. To make your formal announcement, you may want to send personal notes on your own note cards to special relatives and friends, and also put an announcement in the newspaper, alumni newsletter, and/or other publications. There are many people who will want to hear your great news and join the celebration. Enlarge the circle of joy and include them.

OFFERING CONGRATULATIONS

Having received the news of a couple's engagement, you have a wonderful opportunity to add your message of congratulations to the newly declared couple. Join in with words that are affirming, and express your delight.

Message Etiquette

Make your message personal, but keep it consistent with your relationship to the couple. First and foremost, consider their feelings about their new status; then add your voice to their celebration. Your best wishes and hope for their future are key message ingredients.

If you're less than delighted at the news, don't manufacture an effusive message of congratulations. Just send a simple "best wishes" message, or don't send a message at all.

Suggested Messages

OLDER ADULT TO YOUNGER ENGAGED PERSON

- Finding a life partner and a soul mate all in one person is a rare and wonderful thing. We are so happy for you two. Congratulations!
- We wish you great happiness.
- Dreams do come true, it has happened to both of you. Our very best wishes.
- We were delighted to learn about the upcoming wedding. Congratulations on your engagement.
- May all the happiness of two shared lives be yours, [Names].
- Best wishes for your happiness.
- We were delighted to hear of your engagement. Our best wishes to both of you.
- [Name] and [Name], what wonderful news that you have decided to marry. Congratulations!
- Congratulations on selecting a perfect mate; both of you, [Name] and [Name].
- What grand news! Congratulations on your engagement, [Name] and [Name]. I don't know another couple so perfectly in tune with each other.
- A perfectly matched pair, that's what you are, [Name] and [Name].
- [Name], how delighted we were to learn of your engagement to [Name]. Congratulations.

PEER TO YOUNG ENGAGED PERSON

- It's a beautiful thing to consolidate student loans, and life goals, in marriage! Congratulations.
- Oh my goodness! I just heard. You two make a fab pair. Congratulations.
- This news is the best. Congratulations.
- You're just perfect for each other.
- Together you two are perfectly balanced! Radical.
- Wow, fantastic!
- Great news. The very, very best to you two.
- If anyone had to break up our very special girlfriends duo, I couldn't be happier to have it be [Name].
- Really, you two are like a set of perfectly matched diamonds.
- I didn't even guess, but it's wonderful news. Congratulations.
- Mr. Nice Guy, and Ms. Generosity. It couldn't be a better match. It's perfect.
- You two are the perfect complement to each other. What a great match.
- Congratulations! I see happy, happy, happy written all over this marriage.
- Miss Forever Single meets Mr. Quite Wonderful. It's the perfect ending to singlehood! Congratulations, we couldn't be happier for you.

HUMOR

- [Name], wait just one New York minute. It was always our plan that I'd be the one to become engaged first!

   OK, I'll get over it, because I'm completely eaten up

with delight at your wonderful news. I must hear every detail of the proposal, of course. Congratulations to both of you.

- Oh, my goodness! Am I to understand that the woman who was last year's confirmed old maid is this year's betrothed? Amazing. Congratulations!

- This news is sending me straight to the Internet to sign up for e-Harmony! I'm so delighted you've found the perfect mate, [Name]. Congratulations to both of you.

- From all your sorority sisters: a collective congratulations. We'll be waiting to hear all the details. Isn't it amazing that the sister who had no time for socializing—certainly no time for dating—is going down the aisle first! We're all delighted to hear it. The very best to you and [Name].

SPECIAL NOTES

Often parents, siblings, and other relatives are as delighted at the news of their loved one becoming engaged as is the newly engaged person(s). Or, almost. You may add to their joy and celebration by sending a personal message of congratulations. Use either a simple congratulations greeting card and write your personal message inside, or write a note on your own note card. It's sure to increase the joy of the celebration.

- [Name], I can only imagine how delighted you are at the prospect of becoming a mother-in-law. Congratulations to all of you at this time of such happy news.

- I know you've waited a long time to wear that "mother-of-the-groom" label. (Will it be beige for the wedding? Or, will you be a vision of loveliness in celadon? You'll be a vision of loveliness in whatever you wear.) What a delight to hear that the wonderful occasion is here at last.

- You've always made the best sister-in-law. I know you'll be terrific at mother-in-law, too! Congratulations.
- I know you've always been proud of [Name]'s many accomplishments, and are so delighted she's chosen a mate to share her life with. We rejoice with you. Congratulations.
- What an embraceable and lovely couple [Name] and [Name] make. We're thrilled for you. And thrilled for them.

Wedding

Marriage can be one of life's most rewarding experiences. It's been considered one of life's sacred mysteries since very early civilizations. The symbol of the wedding ring, used since ancient Roman times, is thought to symbolize a union for eternity.

Any new couple is enriched if they have a community of family and friends who join together in wishing them well and in supporting them. This is the perfect time to be numbered among those who really care, and to join with the couple, and their families and friends, in celebration as they start this journey of their life together.

Consider, too, spreading the joy by sending a greeting card with your own special message of congratulations to key members of the couple's families.

Message Etiquette

Make your message a warm and loving embrace. Your congratulations should be personal and fresh to be meaningful, but it also needs to be consistent with your relationship with the new couple—in tone and in level of familiarity.

To start putting your thoughts together,

1. Focus on the two people involved and think about a personal characteristic or shared life experience you have had with each partner, or the one you know;
2. Include something about the other partner and something about the wedding, if you can;
3. Connect the couple to their circle of family and friends, and/or to the tradition of marriage;
4. Offer your best wishes for their future life together; and
5. if your greeting card is enclosed with a gift, you may also want to include something about the gift and its application in your message.

A good solution, when you only know one partner well is to first address the partner you know, then include the other. For example: "Jack, from that first day on our Little League Red Robbers team, we've been backup for each other. I'm delighted to welcome you, Kelly, to Jack's team, as well.

"Now, the two of you are moving into a whole new league. How exciting. My best wishes to the new and wonderful 'Team Bonner.' Number me among your inner circle of devout fans. And please know you have my support whenever you need it. Once a Red Robber, always a Red Robber."

If you have any reservations about the choice of this partner, or the marriage, this isn't the time or place to express them. A qualified or restricted message won't play well, either; neither will a false one. If your advice is sought by one of the betrothed, you may feel compelled to give it. Do it privately and verbally, if you must. But know that your statements will undoubtedly become the knowledge of both partners, and probably others, and may cast you in an adversarial role at some point in the future. If you're not an enthusiastic supporter of the union, it is often better not to send a personal written message at all.

QUOTABLE QUOTES

Give all to love;
Obey thy heart . . .
—*Ralph Waldo Emerson,* American essayist and poet

And ruin'd love, when it is built anew,
Grows fairer than at first, more strong, far greater.
—*William Shakespeare,* English dramatist and poet

Let me not to the marriage of true minds
Admit impediments, Love is not love
Which alters when it alteration finds, . . .
—*William Shakespeare,* English dramatist and poet

Chains do not hold a marriage together. It is threads,
hundreds of tiny threads, which sew people
together through the years.
—*Simone Signoret,* French actor

When love and skill work together, expect a masterpiece.
—*John Ruskin,* English author and art critic

Two souls with but a single thought,
Two hearts that beat as one.
—*Friedrich Halm,* Austrian dramatist

Suggested Messages
TO THE COUPLE

- Our best wishes on this great day to two truly wonderful people who share a very special bond.
- We've known two generations of [Family Name]s, and we couldn't be more honored to be seeing you and [Name] enter into this new and exciting role: married couple. Congratulations.
- We are so delighted to join with you, [Name], and [Name], and with both your families at the time of this blessed event in your lives.
- What an important step, and how wonderful that you've both chosen such perfect mates for your married journey.
- May your blessings be many, and all your disagreements be resolved before sunset.
- God bless you and keep you and shine His love fully upon you.
- [Name] and [Name], two hearts united are far stronger than one. Our best wishes that your love will grow sweeter by the day.
- May the beauty of this day flourish and bring forth a uniquely beautiful relationship.
- We wish that the pledges and promises you make this day will be realized in full in your relationship.
- A perfectly matched pair, that's what you are.
- Congratulations, and may God bless and keep you in His perfect love.

- Victories are sweeter, achievements are richer, and even quiet moments are more peaceful when they are shared with the one you love. Our wish for you is that you two will experience it all in abundance.
- Succor each other in difficult times, comfort each other in trying times, and be a true joy to each other always.
- Best wishes for a rich, loving, and long life together.
- May you grow in love and joy; and even in long-suffering, good humor, and in patience! These are the staples of a rich, full, and happy married life.
- Two hearts; one love; joy overflowing. It's the recipe for the wedded bliss we know will be yours.
- Our prayer is that you may come to know fully that the circle of your love is unending.
- Live in the beauty of His love.
- We had hoped for each of you the very best in life; and then you found each other. Perfect.
- Your love and commitment to each other is a wonderful thing to see, and it's a great starting place for a truly happy marriage. Congratulations.
- Happily ever after is really just experiencing the love you share today—one day at a time.
- May your love continue to grow in huge proportions.
- Tolerance is an underrated quality in making marriages harmonious. I've admired this ability you two have in relating to each other. I'm sure your future together is going to be stellar!
- It seems you two have found the right balance of individual identity and couple identity. It's a beautiful thing to see. And it's a formula that insures a rare brand of wedded happiness. Congratulations.

- No, there ain't no mountain high enough to defeat this team. You'll make this one of the best marriages ever!
- You've got our vote for best pairing since John and Abigail Adams. You're a delight to all your family and friends. And you know we all support you 100%.
- Congratulations as you set sail on one of life's most rewarding journeys. I think you have the exact right stuff to make this a perfect union.

TO THE FAMILY MEMBERS

- Congratulations on your wise choice of [Name] to join your family. What a delightful couple he and [Name] make. They seem a perfect pair.
- I'm sure you're completely thrilled to have all the work and headaches of this delightful wedding to execute. Congratulations on the upcoming nuptials. I'm thrilled for you, and with you.
- I know you've wondered if this upcoming wedding would ever happen. And I know you're delighted that at last it's here. Congratulations. I believe I'm nearly as over the moon as you are about it. Please let me know if I can help with any of the details. I'd be particularly good at the guest-book detail, and perhaps making sure guests at every table take a round of photos for the couple's album.
- I'm just a tiny bit envious of [Name] getting to join your family. Does he know exactly what a wonderful thing has happened to him? (I'm thinking here, and salivating, about all that homemade Saturday-night pizza, spaghetti as an appetizer to great family five-course meals, and all

other things Italian. Especially the Italian hugs.) You'll make the perfect mother-in-law. In meeting [Name], I think he'll be a terrific son-in-law, too. I'm sure you can convert him to Italian!

- I'm looking forward to [Name]'s upcoming wedding. Of course, you're far too young to really play the part; but, still, you'll be a gorgeous mother-of-the-bride. Congratulations.
- Congratulations on welcoming a new member into your family circle. He's delightful, and the perfect [Family Name] fit.
- [Name] and [Name], your stock just went up 1,000% with the addition of [Name] to the family portfolio! What a delightful couple [Name] and [Name] make. Your great pride is totally justified. Congratulations.
- Sure, [Name] and [Name] are smart, accomplished, and a perfect match; but what's his handicap on the golf course, and can we depend on him to get our foursome in the winner's circle in the club playoffs? Congratulations, you two, on a daughter superbly parented, and now wonderfully launched into this great adventure called marriage!
- Everything [Name] is screams, "I had the great advantage in life of having two of the best parents on the planet." We know you couldn't be prouder of her, and now of the choice she's made in a life partner. We rejoice with you. You are the Supremes, and stupendous as parents. And great people otherwise, too. Take a bow. We can hardly wait to see what you decide to do now as you start on the next exciting phase of your lives. (After you pull off this wedding, of course.)

WEDDING THANK-YOU NOTES

A very important part of any wedding and marriage is the acknowledgment and confirmation of the support the couple and family have received. Unfortunately, it's often something that is overlooked and/or underexecuted. This leaves people who've given of themselves and their resources feeling un- or underappreciated. Yes, the couple—both partners—needs to write thoughtful messages of thanks to all those who showed their support, and gave gifts. Although latitude is given to the new couple to respond at a more relaxed pace than for other kinds of thanks, the sooner this is done, the more appreciated the receiver of your message will feel.

Family members who planned and orchestrated the wedding should also send personal messages of thanks to those who participated in the ceremony or reception, or helped in some other way. This point of view will be much appreciated by the person receiving the message.

See page 123, "Thank You," for some thought-starters for messages.

Anniversary

Cities have anniversaries, schools have anniversaries, and so do your friends and family—in many stripes and hues. You may add to others' joy and comfort by remembering the special events and markers in their lives on or near the dates on which they commemorate them. There are very happy ones: business anniversaries, and years of employment or service are examples. And there are sad ones: the anniversary of a loss. (See page 55, "Congratulations," for happy occasions; see page 172, "Losses," for comforting message suggestions.)

Your special, personal message will strengthen the bond between you and the recipient, if your message is sensitive and comes
from your heart.

WEDDING ANNIVERSARY

Every married couple delights to know that others remember
and join with them in celebrating their life together. This is the
perfect time to tell the couple how special they are, how inspir-
ing, and how delighted you are to be part of their lives.

MESSAGE ETIQUETTE

Focus on the couple and their relationship, then put yourself
in the picture. Think about the couple first, then your history
with them to get yourself started.

Suggested Messages

- Remember the beautiful bride and handsome groom
  pictured here? [Enclose a picture of their wedding they
  may not have seen.] What a wonderful love story you two
  have created! You inspire us. Congratulations on [num-
  ber] years of happily ever after.
- Building a wonderful relationship is hard work, but you
  two have demonstrated that the love produced is a precious and rare treasure, indeed. And it's golden.
- There are [number] years of precious memories for us
  in celebrating your lives together. Congratulations, and
  thank you both for a fine example of how wonderful
  wedded life can be.
- You've set a very high standard in your exemplary lives
  of wedded bliss. Congratulations.
- Not many of us thought we'd be sending a greeting

celebrating your [number] years of marriage. Thank you both for proving all of us wrong. We rejoice with you.

- We don't know a stronger married team. Your love and lives are both an inspiration and a joy to behold.

- What's love got to do with it? Just about everything, actually, and in full measure. Our best wishes for many, many, many more years of wedded bliss.

- Two very different people; one 24-carat, solid love. You've created a unique recipe for a successful marriage. We applaud you. Congratulations.

- Yes, we were very surprised when you announced your upcoming marriage. We're in awe of the terrific union you've created. Congratulations on another awesome year.

- Melding two unique families, all [number] of you, into one robust and happy household takes the kind of saintly patience and abundant and selfless love few have, but you two demonstrate it in spades. Happy anniversary.

- We marvel at the success you two have produced after blending two households with [number] teenagers. You've proven the impossible is possible; love conquers all. All [number] of you!

- You're both very special and very rare people. And you're a great blessing to all of us who know you. Congratulations.

- Dreams do come true; it has happened to you! Wishes for many more years of wedded joy and happiness.

- No one said love is easy, but it's certainly a joy beyond measure when it's lived the way you two are doing it.

Our best wishes for many, many more happy years to come.

- We'd like to add our congratulations to your celebration.
- Adding one more blissful number to your happy years together is a pleasure for us to observe. Our wishes for many, many more.
- To the best-matched bridge partners we've ever known.
- What a champion tennis doubles team. What a perfectly matched pair. Happy anniversary, Champs.
- As a twosome on the golf course, you're unmatched. As an example of how to be married, you're unparalleled.
- This is us, doing a standing ovation for the superstars of wedded bliss. Bravo, bravo, bravo!
- To answer all those skeptics who said it wouldn't work, stand up and take a bow. You two are a shining example of all that's right in the world of matrimony. Our wishes for many happy years to come.
- In perfect step, in loving harmony. That's you. Happy anniversary.
- Your love has enriched so many lives, ours included. We celebrate with you on this very special day.
- How many years does it take to get it exactly right? It seems you two have known the formula from day one.
- If you could bottle what you have perfected, you'd be very rich. And you are! We feel rich, too, just knowing you! Happy anniversary.
- Our best wishes for cloudless skies, and fair weather ahead.
- Wishes for continued harmony, joy, and wedded bliss.

TO MY BELOVED ON OUR SPECIAL DAY

This is a date you won't want to forget—beware the husband who does! This is a message you'll want to spend some time perfecting on scrap paper before you decide on your final lines to be penned into your special greeting card.

Message Etiquette

Keys to writing a heartfelt message can be found by first focusing on your beloved, and recording those personal characteristics that mean so much to you. Then, too, you'll want to focus on your life together, and name some of the very essential, and very personal, ingredients that bring you joy. You may even want to quote one of the masters to make your point. But a word of caution here: you might try to frame your message in terms of the person first; not only—or first—the value she/he adds to *your* life. Here, I'll illustrate the difference: "You've changed my Saturdays completely. You light them up! What an improvement over my old bachelor days . . ."

While this may be oh-so-true, and perhaps flattering and endearing, it might be better to start with this statement: "You are the most thoughtful and generous spirit I know. It's totally beautiful to see. You demonstrated it again on Saturday when you rearranged your work schedule to spend the afternoon with me. I love spending my Saturdays with you." See the difference?

QUOTABLE QUOTES

Married love between man and woman is bigger
than oaths guarded by right of nature.
—*Aeschylus,* Greek playwright

Can two walk together, except they be agreed?
—*Bible. Amos 3:3*

When you make a sacrifice in marriage, you're sacrificing
not to each other but to unity in a relationship.
—*Joseph Campbell,* American author

Marriage is the perfection which love aimed at,
ignorant of what it sought.
—*Ralph Waldo Emerson,* American essayist and poet

Keep your eyes wide open before marriage,
half shut afterwards.
—*Benjamin Franklin,* American statesman and philosopher

The sum which two married people owe to one
another defies calculation. It is an infinite debt,
which can only be discharged through all eternity.
—*Johann Wolfgang von Goethe,* German poet, playwright, and author

Hail, wedded love, mysterious law, true source
Of human offspring.
—*John Milton,* English author

Suggested Messages

- Let me count the ways I love you: (1) for your strength
in times of trouble; (2) for your calm in stormy weather;
(3) for your gentle patience with our children; (4) for
those thousand and one sweet and thoughtful things
you do. But, mostly, Dear, I love you for who you are,
Mr. Wonderful. [For each point, you may want to add
an example from everyday life.]

- There's no way to really express how deeply I love you. But I'll keep trying because you are the most wonderful person I've ever known.
- You are a truly beautiful person—inside and out. It was a beautiful day when you walked into my life. It's been a beautiful life ever since, [Name].
- Once upon a time when we got married, I couldn't tell you, but I often envisioned you as a wonderful silver-haired grandfather to our grandchildren. And now you are. And what a perfect husband, father, and now grandfather, you've been. I love you so.
- I wake up each day with the realization of how wonderful you are. Let me just start a list I'm sure I'll add to each and every year. First of all, I love you for your patience, like you demonstrated when I [give an incident].
- Another special day to celebrate just how wonderful you are.
- How do I love you? In every possible way.
- You are my beloved. I am yours.
- You are the perfect melody. You make my heart sing with joy. And on key!
- Each new day is a wonder to me: How did I get so fortunate as to have found you? I admire the person you are. You are the love of my life.
- How long will I love you? That's easy: forever.
- My fondest wish is that our love may grow richer with each passing day.
- You mean the world to me because, my dear [Name], you are my world.
- I still have to pinch myself to make sure I'm not dreaming. I am married to the most wonderful man alive.

- I am my beloved's, and my beloved is mine. Oh, what joy!
- This, my dearest, must be the closest two people can come to perfect harmony.
- Imagine a perfect day at 72 degrees, a clear blue sky, and a sun without harmful rays. There's a gentle breeze. And under a towering oak tree, there's a picnic table topped with a red-checkered tablecloth, and set with a huge tin roof sundae with extra fudge chocolate syrup and sprinkles on top. That's how content I feel inside your love.
- I didn't think it possible, but I love you more today than I did the day we got married. Then I only had a glimpse of the wonderful person you would become.
- It took a while, and a whole lot of work to get here, it's true. But you are the visionary and the rock who saw the strong union we could have. Thank you, My Love.
- I searched the world over and found the most handsome, intelligent, and sanguine man alive. Too good to be true? No, my love, that man is you.
- I've had only [number] years to tell you how much I love you. It'll take me at least 1,000 more to fully express how wonderful you are.
- Would I fall in love with you all over again? Yes, oh yes, a thousand times, yes!
- As perfect as this rose are you [delivered with a long-stemmed red rose]. I am in awe of you, afresh, each day.
- How many women are there who can direct a company, run a household, mother [number] children masterfully, and make her mate feel he's the most fortunate person alive? You do it all. You are wonderful. I love you

with all my heart. (And, yes, I'll take out the garbage as
soon as the game is over.)
- Hey, who am I kidding? I'm the luckiest person alive, to
have you as a mate. You're wonderful.

Births and Adoptions

The arrival of a new family member tops the list of life's miracles
to be celebrated. By adding your personal message of congratulations, you will increase the family's measure of joy, and strengthen
your connection to them.

Message Etiquette

If possible, before you select your greeting card and write in
your personal message, gather a little information from a relative
or friend of the family to give you some direction. Learn a fact or
two: Is the baby a boy or girl? What was the baby's birth weight?
Name? Are there any health considerations for baby or parents?
Are there other siblings, and what are their names and ages? Are
there religious beliefs that should be considered? Are there any
other special facts or circumstances you should mention, or
avoid, in your message?

With the answers in mind, select a card that is consistent
with your relationship to the family, and add your personal,
handwritten message. The tone and familiarity will vary, of course,
with your relationship to the family, but you may certainly start
with a general declaration about the advent itself. Something
like: "What a wonderful day, when a baby is born."

Important facts. Next, focus on the parents and the thing
most important to them and this baby. Is it the fact that

they waited a long time for this baby; or, that this is the first child, or the first grandchild; or the first boy, or girl? Is there something extra-special about the birth date, like another family member's birthday, or is it close to a holiday?

Brothers and sisters. Mentioning the new baby's siblings is a great device that makes your message help the whole family celebrate, and will undoubtedly endear you to big brother or big sister. The arrival of a new sibling can be a very difficult transition period for a little star who's had center stage all to herself.

Consider sending a separate and special card to each of the other children in the family. Siblings often struggle with how to feel about this new, tiny interloper who's getting all the attention.

Business associates, colleagues, and social friends. If you are just social friends of one of the baby's parents, or a colleague or business associate, you may want to address the parent you know, making reference to her new role in the context of your relationship; then add a congratulatory phrase or sentence for the other parent: "My congratulations on his new Daddy role to your husband, too."

Other facts to mention. Any unusual circumstances surrounding the birth, like a just-made-it-to-the-hospital arrival, an overdue birth that came at last, a colleague who worked up until hours before the delivery, etc., could be good starting points. Things like a banner announcing the birth flying from the home, an email announcement, the new baby's photos on a Website, or an unusual birth announcement are also good. I just received a birth announcement made up like a rock star poster. And the stamp on the envelope was a photo of the new baby himself! Now there's fodder for a great starting point for my message: "[Parent's Name] and [Parent's Name], congratulations on the arrival of your new rock star, [Baby's Name], complete with his own postage stamp! Wow!"

Other family members. If you are acquainted with other members of the family, you might want to widen your circle of congratulations to include grandparents, and aunts and uncles. Grandparents are often the people who have—hopefully silently—anticipated this event for the longest period of time. And, especially if this is the first grandchild, there is undoubtedly great rejoicing and the desire to share this advent with everyone they know.

QUOTABLE QUOTES

If your children look up to you,
you've made a success of life's biggest job.
—*Anonymous*

Children are God's apostles, day by day
Sent forth to preach of love, and hope, and peace.
—*James Russell Lowell,* American poet and diplomat

Your children are not your children.
They are the sons and daughters of
Life's longing for itself.
—*Kahlil Gibran,* Lebanese-American poet and artist

Children have never been very good at listening
to their elders, but they have never failed
to imitate them.
—*James Baldwin,* American author

There never was child so lovely but his mother
was glad to get him asleep.
—*Ralph Waldo Emerson,* American essayist and poet

Suggested Messages

TO THE PARENTS

- Your little family has just become more perfect. Congratulations on the arrival of your beautiful little bundle.
- A perfect two now becomes three. Oh, what joy.
- We were so delighted to hear about the arrival of your miracle, [Baby's Name]. We rejoice with you.
- It's often said, and oh-so-true, you'll soon not be able to remember life without your new cherub. Congratulations.
- There aren't words to express how happy you've made your dad and me with the birth of little [Name]. We can hardly wait to spoil her totally rotten!
- A brand-new blessing to love. What happy days lie ahead for all three of you.
- Many, many, many are the joys of parenthood. May they all be yours in abundance.
- It's such a blessing to have a perfect baby. And you have two! How doubly blessed you are.
- Congratulations on the birth of this wonderful baby.

- Angels unaware and innocent! What a wonderful gift an infant is. And what a wonderful pair of parents you will be.
- Your much-anticipated event is now your darling [Name]. What a joy!
- Happy days lie ahead.
- How very fortunate young [Baby's Name] is to have been born to two such loving parents.
- I'm sure the angels are rejoicing, as we are, at the birth of little [Baby's Name].
- Welcome, welcome, welcome to our world, little [Baby's Name]. You have had the outstanding good fortune to be born to two perfect parents.

TO THE SIBLINGS

- What did I hear? [Name] is a big brother to a new baby sister, [Name]? Wow! That's terrific. She is going to be so happy to have such a fantastic big brother.
- [Name] has a new baby brother
  A tiny baby so new.
  I think baby [Name] is soooo lucky
  To have a big brother like you!
- How happy you must be, [Name], to be the big sister now!
- Mommy told me that now you, [Name], can count to twenty! There are so many things you'll be able to teach baby [Name] when he gets a bit bigger.
- I hear you have a new baby, [Name], and his name is [Name]. That makes you a big sister. And I think that calls for a special celebration. How about a big sister trip

to the petting zoo on Thursday? Just a special treat for you.

TO THE GRANDPARENTS AND SPECIAL RELATIVES

- Congratulations to you and [Husband's Name]. There have never been a pair of grandparents more up to the task. What a very fortunate baby is [Name]. Does this mean we'll be treated to happy updates at future bridge club meetings?
- I know this is a [title/honor] you wondered if you'd ever receive. Congratulations, Grandmother! It has a very special ring to it, doesn't it?
- You are a superb mother, and I can't wait to see the very special grandmother you'll be. Matchless, I'm sure. Congratulations.
- What wonderful news. Times two! I know you're up for the challenge of being a Grammy to two!
- What wise little souls these babies are to have chosen a grandmother like you. You'll set new Grammy records, I'm sure. Congratulations.
- Of course you're much too young. But how much fun will it be to teach all those sports skills and attend all those games? You'll be great at all of it.

ADOPTION

People who adopt a child are a very special kind of parents, and there are often extreme challenges in getting through the process, as well as a long and difficult period of adjustment. Be sure to tune in to the special circumstances of the new parents, or keep your message general and aimed at the parents if you don't know, or are unsure, how things are going. It's often not appropriate to ask for details.

- Two wonderful, loving people welcome a baby from afar to heart and home. Congratulations on the creation of your new family.
- I can't imagine hearts as big as yours, [Name] and [Name]. You define the word "parents," and I'm proud to call you friends.
- You two are very special people. And now Mom and Dad. Congratulations. As soon as you're settled into a routine, please give a call that you—all three—can come for a picnic. We'd love to meet [Name].
- Very special parents; a very special baby. What could be more wonderful?
- It takes a rare and wonderful pair of parents with a great reservoir of love to select a baby to nurture unconditionally. We are delighted for you, and rejoice with you.
- We don't know, perhaps, the store of love we possess until we select a baby to love. Or, did she select you? Or was it simply a case of recognizing that you were always meant to be parents to this child? We know you feel uniquely blessed. Our best wishes for your happiness— all three of you.
- We can hardly wait to meet the new Miss [Name]. Congratulations!
- We are blessed indeed to have the opportunity to receive this wonderful new family member. We're thrilled beyond words.
- Oh, joy, joy, joy! Our hearts are overflowing with yours.

- Happy days! And years and years to come. Our best wishes for you now that your joy is multiplied.
- Children are the gifts of God! And you have two at once! How blessed you are.
- Every mother, it's said, knows her child, and we're so happy with you that you're now able to embrace your daughter.

Congratulations

You have the power to increase the joy of another person by recognizing her achievement or good fortune. Be generous with your congratulations. Do it with an overflowing heart, and maybe even a little panache. You'll be amazed how good it makes *you* feel, too.

Send a greeting card, and include a handwritten personal message when a friend has been promoted; a colleague has been accepted into a professional association; a teenager has won an academic or sports award; a neighbor has been elected to a political office; a friend has won her designation as master gardener; an author has a new book coming out; and for any other achievement that's noteworthy to the person herself. And even to people you may not know, recognize that person did something special by sending a note.

Message Etiquette

Make your note simple, direct, and focused on the person and her good news. Points to emphasize are her character attributes that made it possible, her steps of preparation, and the endurance or effort it took for her to meet her goal. Knowing a few of the facts, and getting them right in your message, will give what you write the ring of sincerity and authenticity.

QUOTABLE QUOTES

Back of every achievement is a proud wife
and a surprised mother-in-law.
—*Brooke Hays,* American politician and civic leader

The toughest thing about success is that you've
got to keep on being a success.
—*Irving Berlin,* Russian-born American composer

A minute's success pays the failure of years.
—*Robert Browning,* English poet

When men succeed, even their
neighbors think them wise.
—*Pindar,* Greek lyric poet

Suggested Messages

- Wow, you passed the bar exam on the first try. You rock, [Name], Esquire.
- I was in awe when you graduated top of your high school classs, then with honors from college. But a Ph.D. in two years? That's rad. You're a phenom, and you've made us all very proud of you, [Name].
- This is me doing a standing ovation. (Applause. Applause. Cheers. Cheers. Screams from the balcony.) You fully deserve to be accepted into the [Association Name]. You're a pro, and an exceptionally talented [occupation].
- I know how hard you've worked for the "chef" designation. And to graduate from culinary school, win the

"Chop" competition, and land a number-two chef spot at "Flavors"—all in two years—is a testimony to the fact that you just can't be stopped once you make up your mind to achieve something. Congratulations, Chef [Name].

- I saw the announcement of your award online. Do you have any idea how proud of yourself you should be? I'm bursting with pride by association. It's a wonderful award, [Name]. You've created a beautiful thing for a whole lot of people. Congratulations!

- You Rock
  You Roll
  You carry the ball over the goal!
  FOUR TIMES!
  Thanks for being our team's superstar in the game on Saturday. You were sensational.

- I never doubted you for an instant! I've watched you in volleyball practice and games for three years now, and you're a phenom! Congratulations on getting the scholarship to Wright University. I can hardly wait to watch the Wright girls' volleyball team in action.

- Offense, defense, over the fence! What a game you had on Saturday! It was your best performance yet. Congratulations!

- I've just finished reading your master's research paper, and I must say that it's been a very long time since I've read one that contains as much original thinking, and brings such interesting ideas to bear on this topic. Plus, it handles a complete and unbiased view so well. It's more than an outstanding paper, it's the basis for a book! Congratulations.

- Oh, how sweet it was! You belong in the winner's circle. Great job of driving.
- I would be very proud of you if I knew only that you won first place. But I also know that you faced great obstacles along the way, and that makes the win all the more delicious. What a champ!
- You're one of those overnight successes, at last! Right? I happen to know about the 65- and 70-hour weeks, and no vacation for over two years. You're a hero to a lot of people. And a superachiever.
- You only have yourself to thank. What a terrific job of pulling off the fund-raiser. A number of people let you down, I know. But that didn't stop you from creating a star-studded event.
- There won't be another conference like this year's, because there isn't another [Name]. You presented us with the best learning experience we've had for fifteen years.
- What a record, 20 and 4. I'm guessing that record will stand for many a season. Congratulations. You are outstanding.
- Your hard work and perseverance have paid off. Congratulations.
- Good things come to those who keep their eye on the prize and work very hard. We know both are true of you and your dedicated efforts in finishing your licensing requirements.
- We know how hard you worked and the sacrifices you made to achieve your goal to become general manager. That sounds great! We're oh-so-proud of you.

- Congratulations on your promotion. You'll have the support of all of us as you take up your new responsibilities.
- What could be sweeter than turning sweet sixteen? You'll be terrific at it, and at all the new and great things you'll now be able to do. Yes, we heard about the driver's license!
- Your mom has told me that you are now an official babysitter, having passed the Red Cross child-care and safety courses. Awesome!
- I saw your sales numbers for last quarter, and all I can say is, "How did you do it?" Oh, actually, I can say one other thing: "Congratulations. You rock!"
- We just wanted you to know that we appreciate your dedication and willingness to serve as deacon, and we support you in this new ministry.
- There are many ways to serve others, and we are so happy that you will now be heading up the Give Thanks Program.
- Congratulations on hitting in the winning run. Fantastic job!
- Your quilt is absolutely gorgeous. Congratulations on taking the grand prize; you well deserve it.
- You are our favorite overachiever. You're absolutely awesome. Way to go.
- [Name], congratulations on the new living room. You have done a really professional job of decorating.
- Becoming club president is a mixed blessing, I'm sure. But I just wanted to add my congratulations, and say I look forward to being a member during your term of office.

- Brilliant, brilliant, brilliant! That's what I think of the Jansen Report. I've never read a better one.
- New wheels! That's quite an accomplishment for a young man of 17 years old. We know how hard you've worked and saved for this, and we're very proud of you.
- All A's on your report card! Outstanding! This calls for a burger and malt night out. How about Thursday?
- [Name], congratulations on making the semis. What a terrific effort. I certainly wish I owned that wicked forehand!

Rites of Passage and Life Events

Recognizing important life events and significant rites of passage—religious or social—makes them all the more special for the celebrant and her family. It also affirms the connection between you. Don't miss this important opportunity to add your voice to something so precious in the life of someone you know. Go on record as one who notes and honors the milestones that are important in people's lives, who embraces traditions and ceremonies that enrich our lives, and who thinks of others at such important and special times.

Purchase or make a greeting card that is meaningful in its detail to the person, the family, and the event that is being celebrated.

QUOTABLE QUOTES

Train up a child in the way he should go:
and when he is old, he will not depart from it.
—*Bible. Proverbs 22:6*

Feasts must be solemn and rare,
or else they cease to be feasts.
—*Aldous Huxley,* English editor, author, and poet

Friendship should be surrounded with ceremonies
and respects, and not crushed into corners.
—*Ralph Waldo Emerson,* American essayist and poet

Only within burns the fire I kindle.
My heart the altar.
My heart the alter.
—*Buddhist nun*

When humans participate in ceremony, they enter a
sacred space. Everything outside of that space shrivels
in importance. Time takes on a different dimension.
Emotions flow more freely. The bodies of participants
become filled with the energy of life, and this energy
reaches out and blesses the creation around them.
All is made new; everything becomes sacred.
—*Sun Bear,* Native American author

Hearing Mass is the ceremony I most favor during my
travels. Church is the only place where someone
speaks to me and I do not have to answer back.
—*Charles de Gaulle,* French president

Message Etiquette

BIRTH CEREMONIES

This event is often part of a religious ceremony, and it is wise to know what the beliefs of the family are before you decide upon a greeting card and your own personal message. Conversely, if the family won't mark this occasion with a religious reference, it isn't appropriate for you to make one. If you don't know, or don't share, the parents' religious beliefs, select a greeting card that refers only to the joy of adding a new member to the family.

Religious ceremonies after the birth of an infant may be a dedication, a christening, a baptism, a brit milah, a naming ceremony, or a redemption of the firstborn. These all center around welcoming the infant into the family and religious community; and having the parents dedicate themselves to the task of raising their child according to the values of this community.

Gifts for the child are usually appropriate, and afterward there is often a small celebration party or reception for invited family and close friends.

Suggested Messages

- What a wonderful gift you've been given; what a solemn vow you've taken. Our prayers and best wishes to your new family.
- May there be blessings without end upon your wonderful new family, as you welcome little [Name].
- We wanted to join the chorus of well-wishers on this very sacred day of [Baby's Name]'s dedication. She has two wonderful parents who will bring her up in our community of faith.

- We join with you in committing to help bring up [Baby's Name] in the path of faith.
- It's a wonderful day, indeed. You will remain in our hearts and prayers.
- One father, one mother, and one new and tiny life create the sacred mystery of a family. The gift of the precious infant is a solemn trust we know you, [Name] and [Name], take seriously. Please think of us as part of your community of support.
- We're so happy for you as you start on this journey of a family together.
- Such a solemn and sacred day. We rejoice with you for this precious life entrusted to your care.
- May the wisdom of God be yours in the wonderful days and years ahead.
- Our prayer for you, [Name], [Name], and baby [Name], is for joy in abundance.
- [Name] and [Name], we know you will heed the words of the scripture to bring your child up in the way that she should go. What a joyous and blessed time for your new family.
- We're so happy for you at this very special time.

Message Etiquette
FIRST COMMUNION AND CONFIRMATION

This religious ceremony indicates a new step of religious accountability in a child's life and is celebrated as she enters this new phase. Make your greeting match the beliefs and timetable of the family as you join with them in celebrating this new level of faith and accountability. Take your cues from the family, and add your note of greeting in a manner that is consistent with your own faith and your relationship to the celebrant.

Suggested Messages

- [Child's Name], our thoughts and prayers are with you.
- Our hearts are full of joy and rejoicing for you, [Child's Name], on this very special and holy day.
- Sometimes we appreciate very important things in life more as time passes. As much as you are happy about this important day now, I believe it will come to mean even more to you as you become older.
- Happy day! We celebrate with you such an important day in your life.
- Your mother and I did our first communion together. And we've been best friends and sisters in our faith ever since. I am so delighted to see you taking this new step in the church.

Message Etiquette

BAR MITZVAHS AND BAT MITZVAHS

This is the coming-of-age ceremony for Jewish boys (Bar) and girls (Bat), celebrating the youth's new status as an adult member of the congregation.

If you don't share the family's faith, a general note of congratulations is appropriate.

The ceremony is usually followed by a meal and party for invited family and close friends. Gifts are usually given to the celebrant.

Suggested Messages

- Mazel tov! Welcome to the community.
- Your mother told me you have completed all the necessary studies, and are ready for this very special day. We are looking forward to celebrating it with you.
- This is such an important day in your life, [Name]. And we are so very proud of you.
- Your grandmother and mother before you have set fine examples of what a wonderful thing it is to be a young Jewish woman. We all welcome you on this very special day.
- I remember what a tiny baby you were, and how we all wondered if you'd ever grow up. And here you are, ready to become a young woman. We celebrate this very special day with you.
- Congratulations, [Name]. What an exciting time for you.

Message Etiquette

SOCIAL RITES OF PASSAGE

There are a number of social and cultural rights of passage that are an important turning point for a young woman or young man. For young ladies, these include the sweet sixteen and debutante celebrations. There's also the Latino Quinceañera. To remember these with a greeting card and personal note will add significantly to the celebration. Follow the family's lead. Gather a bit of information beforehand, if possible, and add your voice to what will undoubtedly be a very exciting time of celebration.

Suggested Messages

- So soon you are all grown up and stepping out as a young lady. And we are so very proud.
- We all celebrate this important passage with you.
- Playing grown-up was always one of your favorite things, and here you are doing it for the real!
- We just knew you'd turn out fantastically when you took those first steps in Nanna's kitchen and asked for a "cookie." Now you're ready to take the whole cake!
- What exciting days ahead for our dear [Favorite Childhood Nickname]. Does this mean we must now call you [Given Name]? So all-grown-up you've become.
- It's a day of real joy for you, and for all the members of your family, too. (Maybe there's just a tiny bit of sadness at saying good-bye to our curly-headed little darling.) Happy day, our dear Sweet Sixteen.
- It is really cause for celebration: our favorite little niece has now become our favorite young adult niece!

Welcome

Feeling welcome—when all around is new and strange—fills one of our deepest human desires. With a few kind words, you may help a new family member, a neighbor, a member of the club, or an associate feel accepted into the group. Even a new client or customer will be pleased to receive a card with a handwritten message that says, "Welcome, I'm glad you're aboard." You may want to add a little helpful information, too, about the benefits she may now experience. And a sentence about something to anticipate, or the wish for your next meeting, will add another note of comfort and help build anticipation.

Message Etiquette

It's always good manners to introduce yourself to someone new, offer a word of welcome, and include good wishes for her future. You might include a statement about how you've benefited from your membership in the family or organization. It's also nice to make some helpful gesture to make the new member feel at ease. We often forget this, or don't take the initiative, when people join our organizations—or even our families.

Enlarge the tent. Demonstrate a spirit of openness and friendship. Write immediately, and extend an offer to help the individual get acquainted. Close your message with something that anticipates a future meeting and developing relationship.

QUOTABLE QUOTES

You ought to make welcome the present guest,
and send forth the one who wishes to go.
—*Homer,* Greek poet

I had crossed the line. I was free; but there was
no one to welcome me to the land of freedom.
I was a stranger in a strange land . . .
—*Harriet Tubman,* American abolitionist

There is no friend like an old friend who has shared
our morning days, no greeting like his welcome,
no homage like his praise.
—*Oliver Wendell Holmes, Sr.,* American physician and author

Good company and good discourse
are the very sinews of virtue.
—*Izaak Walton,* English author

Suggested Messages

- [Name], welcome to the Garden Club. I've found this not only a great source of information about my plants and flowers, but also a wonderful place to grow a very special friendship. I know you will, too. I look forward to meeting you next week at the meeting. And I look forward to a mutually beneficial relationship in the future.

- I'm so glad you've joined our book club. I welcome your input on the books we'll be discussing. And I believe you'll find it a wonderful avenue to appreciate different points of view on contemporary literature; and also a great way to keep connected to women in the neighborhood. (We always indulge in a local "news" discussion about what's going on in the community before we settle into the book discussion.)

- I was so delighted to hear you'll be joining our [Name of Community] family. Welcome.

- Joining our merry band I'm sure seems a bit strange at first, but I think you'll get into the swing of it very soon. Welcome. I'm so happy to have you as part of our musical [Name of Band or Group] family. I've heard great things about your playing of the alto clarinet.

- We welcome every "New Lifer" member with eagerness, because we all depend upon each other for support in meeting our goals.

- I know there is quite a number of social clubs vying for new members, but I'm absolutely thrilled, [Name], that you joined the Appleton Junior League. This group provides a real way to give back to the community, and also a wonderful way to meet new friends.

- The Business Women's Group is happy to have you join us, [Name]. I've been a member for eight years, and I've learned how to increase my business 500%. I've also made some lifelong friends in the process. I'm sure you'll find the networking and support golden. I'll introduce myself on Thursday; and I invite you to join the networking seminar I'll be running on the 15th. Please give me a call in the meantime, at 555-123-4567, if I can answer any immediate questions. All the networking seminar information is on the Website.

- Welcome to the Navigators. You'll be very glad you joined this lively group. I know I am. See you next meeting.

- Welcome to the ASJA. The fact that you've worked to meet the requirements for membership says that you are a serious professional. We have a regional group I'm sure you'll be very excited about interacting with, too. We'll be meeting at my house on the 15th, and I'll be emailing you all the details in a couple of days.

- It's members like you, [Name], who've made Family Support Annons the great source of succor and shelter from the storm that it is for our members. Welcome. You'll be assigned to your own FSA group in the next week, and we'll have a whole chapter meeting on June 1. I know you'll soon wonder how you ever made it through the week without FSA. We're so happy to have you as part of our support group.
- Welcome to the Press Club! We're delighted to have you. I'm sure you've been told that you are now a member of the oldest press club in the region. It's both a professional and a social club, and I suggest you take advantage of the New Members' Tea on Tuesday to learn all the benefits that are at your disposal. I'll introduce myself then. I invite you to call me if there's anything you'd like to know in the meantime. (Most general questions are answered on the FAQ on the Website.)

New Home

So many things go into making a house a real home. Key is each and every happy memory that is built into our experience with the family within its walls. But also in the community surrounding its walls. You can add to the warmth and help in the transforming process by adding your hopes and wishes to the family who has moved to that new address, or, who has renovated an old one.

Message Etiquette

This is a happy message of congratulations and welcome. Send your message as soon as you know the person has made a move into the new house. Include some of the details and positive aspects of the move, the new location, the new house, and the new neighborhood and community. Then offer your best wishes for the future. A small gift of welcome—especially something like an afternoon tea mug, tea bags, and cookies—can go a very long way toward establishing a rewarding relationship. Timing, too, is an important aspect of putting real legs on your message of welcome.

QUOTABLE QUOTES

He is happiest . . . who finds peace in his home.
—*Johann Wolfgang von Goethe*, German poet, playwright, and author

The ache for home lives in all of us, the safe place
where we can go as we are and not be questioned.
—*Maya Angelou*, American writer and poet

Whoever makes home seem to the young dearer
and more happy, is a public benefactor.
—*Henry Ward Beecher*, American clergyman and reformer

You are a king by your own fireside,
as much as any monarch on his throne.
—*Miguel de Cervantes*, Spanish author

In love of home, the love of country has its rise.
—*Charles Dickens*, English author

Stay, stay at home, my heart, and rest;
Home-keeping hearts are happiest.
—*Henry Wadsworth Longfellow*, American poet

Suggested Messages

- A home is four walls where love and care live. We're so happy you're all settled now in your new house. It is, I hear from your mom, a lovely home in a wonderful school district. Best wishes to you and your family for a rewarding and growing future there. We'll miss you here, but hope to see you next summer when we come to your new home in [City].
- Blessings in abundance upon your new home. May you be exceptionally happy in it.
- Such good news that you've selected a new home. It sounds delightful, and we'll look forward to visiting when you're settled.
- Love, laughter, joy, and peace be yours in your new home.
- That first home is always very special. May yours be filled with love and laughter and many happy events that build treasured memories.
- May the glow of your love fill your new home with warmth—even if the furnace doesn't work.
- I can hardly wait to see your new home. You do such an excellent job with decorating. It's sure to be fit for *House Beautiful*'s pages.
- I know you're delighted to be moving from a house into a condo, though it's always with a tiny bit of regret to leave the place where so many memories live. But I also know you'll take the love and laughter that were such a part of your life there, and install both, in abundance,

in your new home. Best wishes. I'm sure you'll be care-free as a bluebird in your new condo, and wonder why you waited so long to make the change.

- You've picked a lovely new home. Happiness to all of you within its walls.
- Our congratulations to the [Family Name]'s in their brand-new home. May it be a place of serenity, sunshine, and much happiness.

PART THREE

Holiday Messages

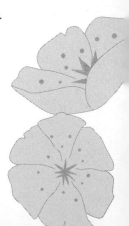

Holidays of all color and stripe enrich the lives of those
who celebrate them. They bring families together, create
traditions, and foster fond memories.

Spread the joy by sending a greeting card with a special
handwritten note to friends and relatives at holiday time.
The act will make you present and connect you to each
other's lives. But before you do, it's important to
know—in at least a bit of detail—the beliefs of those
you're sending a message to, in order to be sure your
message will add to their celebration, and not offend.

New Year's Day

When a New Year is approaching, it's the perfect time to establish the habit of connecting with those you may not have been in touch with for a while. This is a time of renewing. You can start by sending a greeting card with good wishes, and add your own personal message.

Often, wishes for the New Year are part and parcel of season's greetings sent for the religious holidays that occur at the end of the year. But for those friends and relatives who don't celebrate religious holidays, and for others, such as business associates, you may want to send a New Year's greeting card with your own personal handwritten message.

Message Etiquette

Make your message personal by starting with the recipient, and include something about your good wishes for her and her goals and plans for the New Year. Write your message on the greeting card in a personal way. You may also want to include a shared experience or memory, and suggest a plan for a future get-together.

QUOTABLE QUOTES

Ring out the old, ring in the new,
Ring happy bells, across the snow:
The year is going, let him go;
Ring out the false, ring in the true.
—*Alfred, Lord Tennyson,* English poet

Year's end is neither an end nor a beginning but a going on, with all the wisdom that experience can instill in us.
—*Hal Borland,* American author

Then sing, young hearts that are full of cheer,
With never a thought of sorrow;
The old goes out, but the glad young year
Comes merrily in tomorrow.
—*Emily Miller,* American musician

Youth is when you're allowed to stay up late on New Year's Eve. Middle age is when you're forced to.
—*Bill Vaughan,* American author

Suggested Messages

- Our wish is that this will be a five-star year for you, though it would be hard to top the stellar year you just had!
- Happy New Year. I'm eager to hear about your plans for this year's marathon. Let's do arrange to spend a little time together for a visit to catch up sometime in January.

- It's always wonderful to start out with a clean slate. Happy New Year, and may [new year] be filled with all your heart's desires.
- Yes, we're wishing you the best of the best for this new year.
- Twelve new months of all good things to the [Family Name]s.
- We're sending good thoughts for a fantastic year to come.
- Best wishes for a healthy, happy, and peaceful New Year to you and yours. We're so happy to know that [Name] is back from Iraq, and safe at home again. That, alone, makes the prospects for the New Year very, very bright.
- I know you're hard at work on your goals for the New Year. Just let me say that I recognize you accomplished a great deal last year. I can hardly wait to see what you have on your New Year goals list.
- Wishes for a peaceful, prosperous, and joyous New Year. With that new baby, [Name], we already know it will be crammed with lots of wonder and joy! Happy, happy, happy [year]!
- Yes, it's that time again, for resolutions. You're always so good at that—and at accomplishing them. Can you get together in February in New York for dinner, a theater night, and our annual resolution review? If I remember last year's, you had achieved 100% of yours, and I had yet to achieve the first item on my list! This year I'll do better. Promise.

Valentine's Day

Remember the early grade-school buzz and bustle about Valentine's Day? Maybe your classroom was alight with a big red box affixed with lacy paper doilies, or decals, or old pasted-on cards from years past. The atmosphere—as I remember mine—was alive with anticipation for a couple of weeks before the day. When the day finally arrived, the fun started early, and lasted until the very last Valentine was handed out.

Then, of course, everyone who has lived through a first romance that was in play over a Valentine's Day remembers the thrill of celebrating with that very special someone. The Valentine's Day greeting card, the personal handwritten message, and perhaps a gift or flowers, were prerequisites for the occasion.

But this special day is no longer just for the romantically smitten. It's also an appropriate time to widen the circle of your affection by sending caring messages to friends and relatives. Young people, especially, will enjoy a special Valentine's Day card with an added surprise of a balloon, stickers, or a lollipop.

Message Etiquette

Using broad brushstrokes of love and care, select cute, clever, sincere, and charming valentines, keeping your recipient clearly in mind. Humorous ones can also be lots of fun. Sincere and charming ones are appropriate for almost everyone on your list. In several families close to me, even the dog gets a valentine— often written on, or attached to, a rawhide chew.

Don't forget to write your own personal message. This is even a great time to exercise your poetry muscle. (Yes, you have a poetry muscle.)

QUOTABLE QUOTES

All mankind love a lover.

—*Ralph Waldo Emerson,* American essayist and poet

The lover is made happier by his love
than the object of his affection.

—*Ralph Waldo Emerson,* American essayist and poet

It is easier to be a lover than a husband for the simple
reason that it is more difficult to be witty every day
than to produce the occasional bon mot.

—*Honoré de Balzac,* French author

A word to lovers: this is the time to express what's in your heart, and believe that love will last. Make it uniquely personal by capitalizing on your history and relationship. Untether your emotions, be unguardedly honest, and even include something unexpected—a surprise. Also see Love Notes (and Letters), on page 150.

Suggested Messages

- Valentine's Day is just one more very special day to say to you, [Name], that you are very simply the love of my life.
- [Name], every day I love you more.
- You're Grandma's sweetie pie, Valentine.
- Roses are red, violets are blue; I never cared much for Valentine's Day, until there was you!
- Twinkle, twinkle, my Valentine Star. Oh, how wonderful you are!

- A-tisket, a-tasket; here's another valentine for your basket. What a wonderful Valentine you are.
- How big is my love for you? Bigger than the moon and the stars and all the way back.
- Hickory, dickory, dock. You really ring my bell, and rock my world.
- [Name], no one can ever fill the spot you hold in my heart. No one but you!
- Why do I love you? Because you are perfect, that's why.
- Once upon a time there was a wonderful little girl named [Name], and I just want to say Happy Valentine's Day.
- You are my Valentine, [Name].
- Nowhere on earth is there another Valentine half as buff as you.
- Perfect, perfect, perfect in every way. That's what you are.
- I love you just the way you are. (My list of desired changes will arrive under separate cover.)
- Best friend, lover, and soul mate. That's you. What could be more perfect, My Valentine? Maybe the evening together? Just the two of us? That would be more perfect.
- You're the banana in my split; the hot fudge on my sundae. You're simply yummy, Valentine.
- This is our [number] Valentine's Day. I had no idea you would be [number] years more perfect today, than all those years ago, Valentine.
- What is a Valentine? It's a perfect pulse, and beating with life. That's you, Valentine.
- Am I a poet? Hardly. And my love for you is like, way beyond words, anyway.

- You're in my blood, and in my heart. And in my life forever.
- Here's to the best husband I'll ever have! (I'll never want another.)
- Here's a big hug and a kiss for my little Valentine.
- My heart's desire? Candlelight, soft music, and a romantic dinner. Or, maybe just time with you, My Valentine.
- Be my Valentine, this day and for every day for the rest of our lives.
- Sugar and spice and everything nice, that's what you are made of, Valentine.
- Won't you be my Valentine? I'll sing it all day through. If you won't be my Valentine, I'll be really, really blue. It's true.
- Oh, the places we'll go now, Valentine.
- [Name], I really didn't know what love was until I met you.
- You sweep me off my feet, Valentine.
- Every day is a celebration with you, my love.

St. Patrick's Day

You don't even have to be Irish to join in on the festivities of celebrating this special day. And on a day like this, so alive with celebration, isn't everyone Irish anyway?

Message Etiquette

Picking out a special card for those who are or love the Irish can add to the happy celebration of this special day. Embrace the day, and all those who celebrate it. It's as good an excuse as any to extend a personal greeting of friendship and frolick.

QUOTABLE QUOTES

May the road rise up to meet you,
May the wind be always at your back.
May the rain fall gently on your fields.
May the sun shine warmly on your face.
And may you be in heaven three days
before the Devil knows you're dead.
—*Anonymous*

Suggested Messages

- Hoorah for the Irish!
- If you don't count the fatalism, love for strong drink, or black moods, being Irish is as good a reason to celebrate as any I can think of on this very special day.
- Today we're all Irish; raise a glass!
- Come join us for some Irish coffee, Irish poetry, a few Irish fiddles and songs, some Irish dancing, and nothing—but the Guinness—that's like an Irish wake.
- From one of Dublin's sons to another, let's make a bloomin' green day of it!
- Thank God we're Irish!
- It's a great day to adopt the country of Ireland and celebrate!
- You've got to love a country where the hills are always green, the drink is chewable, and the music makes you want to dance!
- Tip your hat to Ireland. Isn't it grand to be Irish?
- A fiddling good time on this very special Irish day.

- Hoorah for the Irish! Let's raise a glass, and toast all her lovely sons, close to home and in faraway lands, where they're still close to the heart.
- May the road rise up to meet you, and take you back to the best of all it means to be Irish.

Easter

This is a wonderful time of year for those who share the Christian faith to celebrate the gift of eternal life. Remembering this day that commemorates Jesus Christ's resurrection after His death, you may also want to include a memory or two of past Easters you've shared with the recipient. Often, families of the Christian faith make this a special time to get family, friends, and those who share their faith together for a special Easter breakfast or dinner—with or without a special religious ceremony.

For children, especially, some other traditions have been woven into the celebrations for this day: Easter baskets, Easter egg hunts, and the Easter Bunny. You may want to include comments about the day's activities and memories of these things from Easters past.

Message Etiquette

The common greeting for Christian denominations is "Happy Easter," or "Have a blessed Easter," but you may select an adult greeting card that contains good wishes for the day. For those of Eastern Orthodox faith (Pascha), which lasts forty days symbolizing the exodus from Egypt to the Pentecost, the greeting is: "Christ is risen." The response is: "Truly He is risen."

Light or humorous cards with one of the traditional themes may be selected for children.

QUOTABLE QUOTES

He is not here: for he is risen, as he said.
—*Bible. Matthew 28:6*

Suggested Messages

- May the joy of this season be yours.
- Happy Easter in this season of hope.
- [Name], have a blessed Easter.
- A happy and joyous Easter to you all.
- We rejoice with you in this most blessed of seasons.
- Happy Easter from our house to yours.
- May the hope and joy of Easter live in your hearts.
- Warmest wishes for an Easter filled with the joy of having your family close.
- May the joy of the risen Christ be yours today and every day.
- I'm hoping, [Child's Name], that you'll have lots of fun filling your Easter basket. Maybe you'll find five eggs on the egg hunt on Saturday. Do you think you will find that many?
- Remember last year when Marley got into your Easter basket and ate all the jelly beans? What a rascal that dog is. Happy Easter.
- Hippity hop, hippity hop. This little bunny says happy Easter to you.

- Coloring Easter eggs, wearing a special dress, and maybe even brand-new shoes? Wow, what a wonderful day that will be. Then you'll come to Grandma and Grandpa's house for a very special dinner, and we'll go to church for our Easter Cantata. I can hardly wait. Happy Easter, [Name].

May Day and Spring

May Day started in the British Isles as a pagan festival of the Druids even before the birth of Christ. Beltane, as it was called, signaled the start of the second half of the year. The custom of setting a new fire, which was thought to lend life to the new springtime sun, was also a ceremony of purification and good luck.

The Roman occupation of the British Isles brought the five-day end of April and first of May celebration, which included the worship of Flora, the goddess of flowers. Eventually, the two traditions became what we know as May Day. Puritans who migrated to America didn't endorse this celebration because of its pagan beginnings, so it never became popular in the United States.

In Europe, however, May Day celebrations of spring, or solstice, are alive and well. Festivities involve singing and dancing around a Maypole tied with bright, colorful streamers or ribbons, and moving in a pattern that weaves these streamers together. Making daisy or other flower chains and wreaths, choosing a May queen, and picking flowers and making May baskets—which are hung on doorknobs of family, neighbors, and friends—are all part of British and European practices for the day. In France, the May Tree became the Tree of Liberty, a symbol of the French Revolution, and has its own set of festivities.

Message Etiquette

In this season of new beginnings, awakenings from a deep sleep of winter, and the birth of new life, send your messages of renewal and hope to neighbors, family, and friends who will not be offended by the pagan origin of celebrating May Day. You may want to write something about your wish for the renewal this season brings. You may even want to include a packet of seeds with your hopes of seeing the new flowers.

QUOTABLE QUOTES

No Winter lasts forever, no Spring skips its turn. April is
a promise that May is bound to keep, and we know it.
—*Hal Borland,* American author

April showers bring May flowers.
—*Anonymous*

Hard is the heart that loveth nought in May.
—*Geoffrey Chaucer,* English poet

April is the cruelest month, breeding
Lilacs out of the dead land, mixing
Memory and desire, stirring
Dull roots with spring rain.
—*T. S. Eliot,* American poet and author

Suggested Messages

- Isn't it great, that smell of spring in the air? Best wishes for the renewal in your life that this month brings.
- May the warm breath of spring blow gently on your hearts and home.
- Spring is filled with promise, and that's our wish for you.
- All things are possible in spring. Blessings on your home.
- Our love to you as the earth and all the flowers awaken with the promise of new life.
- As you dance around the Maypole celebrating the big thaw, may all the hope of the season bloom in your hearts, even if the mud does stick to your new Sunday shoes.
- May the warm sun and spring showers fall gently on you and all your household.
- Send up a shout of joy for spring is here! At last!
- As the birds return and the grass turns green, we wish you all the renewed and bright hope of this new season.
- Spring is synonymous with thinking of you in your garden, raking, planting, and smiling! Thanks for this recurring image of spring. And best wishes for a garden even more beautiful than last year's. Happy Springtime.
- April showers bring May flowers, but who brings the weeds?
- Happy Springtime, as we'll all burst forth from our long winters of shut-in silence and gray snow.

Mother's Day

The ancient Greeks honored Rhea, the mother of the Gods, each spring. Then in the 17th century, in England, early Christians introduced a day to honor Mary, the mother of Jesus. Later, this day was officially expanded to include a day to honor all mothers, and it became known throughout the British Isles as Mothering Sunday, and was celebrated the fourth Sunday of Lent.

Over time these traditions melded into one. But it didn't take hold in the United States until after the Civil War, when Julia Ward Howe, who wrote "The Battle Hymn of the Republic," took up the cause to create Mother's Day Peace Proclamation against war, or what in 1872 she called, "Mother's Day for Peace."

Although Howe failed to get a national day established, she planted the seed. In 1858, Ann Marie Reeves Jarvis initiated "Mother's Friendship Day," to help improve sanitation conditions in the Civil War by teaching women nursing and sanitation skills. Her daughter, Anna Jarvis, finally succeeded in establishing Mother's Day on May 10, 1908, to honor her own mother.

Today, the holiday to honor mothers is celebrated around the world.

Message Etiquette

Our first and most important lessons about love and caring came from our mothers. To bring your loving Mother memories to light and page, focus on the person your mother is, and come up with something very special to express the contents of your heart. You'll undoubtedly want to write some draft notes to work out your message before penning it into your greeting card.

You might want to add a "Love Coupon" or two that says how much you care. Make your gift something that will last the whole year, like coffee with you once a week on Friday mornings, a series of plays or performances you will attend together, or once-a-month shopping trips for the two of you.

You may want to help the children write an I-Love-Grandma card, too. It will be a wonderful life lesson for the children on how to write loving notes.

QUOTABLE QUOTES

God bless my mother; all that I am,
or ever hope to be I owe to her.
—*Abraham Lincoln,* American president

Oh, what a power is motherhood, possessing
A potent spell. All women alike
Fight fiercely for a child.
—*Euripides,* Greek playwright

The mother-child relationship is paradoxical and, in a sense, tragic. It requires the most intense love on the mother's side, yet this very love must help the child grow away from the mother, and to become fully independent.
—*Erich Fromm,* German psychoanalyst and social theorist

Suggested Messages
- Thank you for being my mom.
- When Moms were passed out, I got the best one!

- I'm the luckiest kid ever, to have a Mom like you!
- Roses are red, violets are blue,
  There'll never be another Mom half as wonderful as you.
  <u>You're Number One.</u>
- I am, and always will be, your biggest fan; I'm so happy you're my mom.
- Thanks for showing me what a truly wonderful Mother is. I'm so glad you're mine. I was just thinking about that day when I was six . . . [fill in with personal story]
- What did I do to deserve such a terrific Mom? It was just a divine mercy that God looked the whole universe over, and sent me to the Number One Choice.
- You got "the difficult years"; I got unconditional love. I'm thinking I got the best part of the bargain, and the best Mom ever.
- Thanks for loving me, and for always letting me be me. Remember the day you picked me up from school and I was wearing . . . [fill in with personal story]
- It's a rare Mom, I'm thinking, who calmly suggests decision options, then watches her child make mistake after mistake, and still resists the impulse to say "don't do that"; and, later, "I told you so." Giving good guidance, and then letting me make my own decisions (often spelled m-i-s-t-a-k-e-s) has taken a Mother lode of love, courage, and patience. Thank you for all the wisdom you've exercised on my behalf. I love you.
- I've always admired your courage, but never more than when . . . [fill in with personal story]
- You are everything I admire. Let me just count a few . . . [fill in reasons]

- I could search the whole world over and never find a better Mom.
- Number One Mother, Best Friend! That's what you are to me.

Message Etiquette

STEPMOM

Writing to a stepmom should reflect what your relationship with her has become over your time together. Find a true and genuine tone by first focusing on who she is, and then expressing your appreciation and your relationship genuinely.

Suggested Messages

- Loving the kid who comes as part of the package is a tall order, I finally realize. It took me awhile, it's true. Thank you for hanging in there. I've come to love you in a very special way.
- You've turned our ragged foursome into a wonderful family. Thank you, Mom Too. We love you.
- Any Mom can love her own flesh-and-blood children, I believe. It takes a very, very special Mom to love the little troublemakers she inherits with the man she loves. You've been a true Mother, and we all love and appreciate you.
- Thank you for all your love and caring. Happy Mother's Day.
- I can't say your name without thinking "courage" and "determination," which you've displayed from the very first day you walked into our unhappy home, and turned on the bright light of your love. You're a wonderful person, and we are all so very happy Dad found you. We love you.

- Stepmoms are called on to love in very extraordinary ways. And your love and caring have been extraordinary, indeed. With love, Mom, on Mother's Day.

Message Etiquette
MOTHER-IN-LAW

This is a great opportunity to embrace your mother-in-law; to reinforce—or forge—your bond with this very important Mother in your family. It's also a golden opportunity to help teach your children to love and respect their grandmother. The best starting place may be your shared love for your husband. Perhaps, too, you will be able to express how you've grown to appreciate and care for your mother-in-law for who she uniquely is. That would be the best Mother's Day message, if you express it well.

Never neglect this relationship. Don't relegate it to the territory of your spouse. It's the stuff truly happy families are made of.

Suggested Messages
- Only a wonderful woman like you could have raised such a thoughtful and considerate son. I thank you with all my heart. I love you. Happy Mother's Day.
- Happiness is having a Mother by marriage like you.
- I've so enjoyed coming to know and love the delightful person you are.
- Thank you for your loving care and support. Happy Mother's Day.
- Loving the same man—your son, my husband—gives us a very special bond. Thank you for helping to make him as perfect as he is. And thank you for opening your heart and life to me, and welcoming me into your family.

- I know you will always be [husband's Name] mother. Thank the stars above. Thank you for being the loving glue that has helped us build this loving family.
- It's a special day to say a special thank you for the difficult job you've done so well. Happy Mother's Day.
- Since having children, I've come to appreciate what a difficult job motherhood is. Thank you for a job well done.
- May all your wishes for this day come true.
- We all value the Mom who stood for such great principles, and worked to instill those values in her son.
- Happy Mother's Day, Mom.
- Thank you for being the perfect Mother-in-law. You completely rock.

Message Etiquette
GRANDMOTHER

There really aren't enough Moms in the world. So, while you still have her to cherish, be sure to include your grandmother, and your children's grandmother(s), on this special day. Consider, even, creating a tradition of making it a special and big celebration—one that really honors the role of Mothers in our lives. It will pay handsome dividends of love, bonding, and caring. It will even help grow much more loving children.

This is the ideal time to help train children to express their appreciation for their mothers and grandmothers, too. They will learn from your example. Involve your children in both writing a special message, and in helping to create a true and loving celebration.

Suggested Messages

- Grandma, on this Mother's Day I just want to say a very special thank you for mothering two generations of children.
- Grandmothers are really always mothers, and you'll always have that very special place in my heart.
- A very special Mother's Day wish to the Grand Mother of them all!
- Best wishes to our wonderful Grandmother on Mother's Day.
- My earliest wonderful memories are of the days I spent at your house canning peaches. I remember you letting me stand on the little stool and "peel," though I'm sure I ate far more peaches than ever got into the jars. Do you think that's why I had that terrible stomachache?
- I remember when I stayed at your house while Mom and Dad went to England, and when I was homesick you said, "We'll just pretend I'm your mom for a little while." It was fun to play pretend, and I've always thought of you as my second mom, Grandma. And I've always loved you for all your caring ways.

Message Etiquette

OTHER MOMS

Expanding the circle by sending greetings to those women who have played an important mothering role in your life can really make this a special day—both for the Mom(s) and for you. Imagine the joy you will spread! This could be the start of honoring acts of mothering everywhere. That would be a very, very good thing, indeed.

Suggested Messages

- It takes a very special person to have a mother's heart, and you, [Name], have more heart than any Mom I've known. I just wanted to tell you how I appreciate you on this day of honoring the Mothers in our lives. That's you! Happy Mother's Day.
- Wishing you joy on this special Mother's Day.
- Thank you for all your loving, caring acts over this past year. Happy Mother's Day.
- A Mother's heart is what you have, and such a caring spirit. Thank you for all your loving ways, and all your acts of care and concern; you define the word "Mother."
- "What would [Name] say, or do?" I ask myself in times of tough decisions. Thanks for all your mothering advice, and a very happy Mother's Day to you.
- Best wishes for a true Mother's Day celebration.
- The most important job in the world, and only a single day to celebrate. Thank you for doing such a super Mom job. Happy Mother's Day.

Father's Day

The tradition of this day may date back four thousand years to a clay tablet in Babylon, and a boy named Elmusu, who wrote a message to his father, wishing him good health and a long life. Like many traditions, Father's Day has been influenced by religious and cultural celebrations over the centuries and around the world. The Catholic celebration of St. Joseph's Day on March 19, for example, became the observed date in many Catholic countries. In the United States, Father's Day was celebrated first on June 19, 1910, in Spokane, Washington. The driving force behind it was Sonora Smart Dodd, who wanted to honor her father, Henry Jackson Smart, who raised her after her mother's death. In 1924, President Calvin Coolidge established the third Sunday in June as the official date for Father's Day; and in 1972, President Richard Nixon made it a permanent national observance on that day.

Message Etiquette

Whether your dad finds verbalizing his feelings difficult or not, he'll still appreciate—though he may not say so—your heartfelt expression of love and caring on this special day. You may want to express it by detailing how much you appreciated a shared experience with him. List some specific things. And you may want to think about arranging a special outing as part of your Father's Day celebration.

QUOTABLE QUOTES

It is a wise father that knows his own child.
—*William Shakespeare,* English dramatist and poet

Now, we've made the revolutionary discovery that children have two parents. Once, even the kindly Dr. Spock held mothers solely responsible for children.
—*Gloria Steinem,* American feminist and author

The fundamental defect of fathers . . . is that
they want their children to be a credit to them.
—*Bertrand Russell,* English philosopher and author

Lucky that man whose children make his happiness
in life and not his grief, the anguished
disappointment of his hopes.
—*Euripides,* Greek playwright

Suggested Messages

- You get the Father-of-the-Year Award. You're the best. Happy Father's Day.
- Here's a "Super Dad" badge for you. It's not just for today, but for all the days of the year.
- To a Dad who listens. And gets it. Happy Father's Day.
- Thank you for setting the example of good character: truthfulness, honesty, and loyalty. And all the other attributes you have in spades that make you Dad of the Year.
- There are lots of ways to be special. You seem to have mastered all of them. Happy Father's Day.
- Where did I learn to bait a hook, swing a bat, throw the long ball, and always tell the truth? One look in the mirror will show you the person who has directed all my ways. Thank you, Coach! You're the best. I love you, Dad. Happy Father's Day.
- It's a joy that you are present in my life, and I love you. Happy Father's Day.
- Here's to the new Dad, who'll do the title proud!
- To the man who takes his Dad role very seriously. And

has achieved first chair in that role. Happy Father's Day.

- Thanks for teaching me how to be a man. And a Dad. You're the best.
- Remember those late nights mastering the square knot, learning the allegiance to the flag, rehearsing the Sousa march for trumpet? I wasn't the best student, but you get an A+ in Dad conduct!
- <u>Hero</u> and <u>Friend.</u> Those are two words that mean "Dad" to me! Happy Father's Day.
- Sure, I'll be a geek just like you. And proud of it. Happy Father's Day.
- Today, tomorrow, and for every other day—you're the best Dad ever.
- In nearly all my fondest childhood memories, you're my starring hero. It's still true today. Thanks for all your great feats of fatherhood. I love you, Dad.
- Who's the best Dad of them all? No contest. It's you, Dad.
- In the Best Dad competitions, you get "First Place."
- For all the games of catch, Little League, and high school sports, you were right there. And you still are. Thanks for being the Very Present Dad.
- My friends always seemed to think you were a great Dad, a feeling I didn't share when I was rebelling against your family rules, and being grounded for it! Now I realize how important those rules were, and how wise you were. And are. Or, have you just smartened up in the last [number] years?
- I value the values you taught me <u>now</u>; even though I didn't at the time you introduced them. Thanks for

insisting on the important principles. I'll try to do the same when I'm the Dad, and you're the Granddad.

- Now that I can look back and see the effect of those rules, I want to thank you for sticking to your guns. Happy Father's Day.
- I love you, Dad.
- How did I get so lucky as to get such a great Dad? I don't know, but I'm thankful for you every day. Happy Father's Day.
- Was I a teenager under your roof for only six years? My goodness. It seemed like <u>forever</u> at the time; and now I treasure that time and all I learned from you. Happy Father's Day.

Message Etiquette
STEPDAD

It needn't be formal or long, but don't overlook your stepdad on this special day. Focus on him, his character and attributes. You might even start with a shared memory, or two. It may make your job a bit easier if you try a little exercise of reframing: what was he feeling when he met the kid you were and began to try to create a place for himself in your family?

Suggested Messages
- Stepdads often have a really tough job. You did. Thanks for doing it with grace and style, Dad.
- Sure, you're Dad Two. And Dad, too. But you're also Number One! Thanks for all your love and care, and perseverance to "make it" in this family. Happy Father's Day.
- I appreciate all your patience and long-suffering with me

during the first years of our relationship. Who knew we'd become so close? Happy Father's Day.

- Stepdads and stepchildren: it's always a recipe for harmony. Not. But you are truly an outside-the-lines kind of guy, and a wonderful, stand-up Dad. Thank you for your love and patience. And thanks for creating the loving family we've become.

- <u>Stepdad and friend,</u> can anyone really put those three words in the same sentence? I can, and mean them from the bottom of my heart. Happy Father's Day.

- Rose are red, violets are blue, there was never a better Dad than you!

- I'm so proud to call you Dad.

- You've never tried to replace my father. You were always just your own special brand of a very special Dad. Thank you. Happy Father's Day.

Message Etiquette
GRANDFATHER

Be sure to include your grandfather, and your children's grandfather(s), when sending greetings for this special day. Plan some special honoring act or celebration, if possible.

It's a perfect time to help the children learn how important it is to love, appreciate, and honor those who love us. And Grandpa will welcome their drawings, memories of times together, and notes of love.

Suggested Messages
- There never was a better Dad than you, Grandpa!
- I just want to thank you, Gramps, for being the kind of

Dad who takes his son, and now grandson, on all kinds of adventures. I count myself the luckiest kid alive!

- Who's the first person I want to share a success with? It's you, Grandpa, because you're so special to me.
- Who's never too busy to listen; always has a minute to talk about a problem? That's my wonderful Grandfather, that's who. Happy Father's Day.
- Thanks for practicing on Dad, and being a perfect Grandpa to me.
- For all the wonderful memories of hikes, and biking, and fishing, and camping out. You're the very best, Gramps.
- There aren't enough special days, so I want to add you to the Father's Day list. I love being your grandson. I'm very thankful I got you for a Grandfather! You're the absolute best and most awesome ever.

Independence Day

Traditions that help define who we are should have an important place in our lives. Remembering and celebrating them helps reinforce the values we hold dear. They add warp and weft to the tapestry of our experience. They add depth to our lives. And they create identity and pride for us and others with whom we share them.

Message Etiquette

Send an Independence Day greeting card with your personal message to anyone who holds her citizenship in this country especially dear. A new citizen, certainly; and a person who immigrated here to be free of political persecution, absolutely.

It's also a great time to remember and celebrate our national heritage by sending out greetings to those who are actively defending our country in the armed forces. And certainly a very personal greeting and thanks should be sent to any who have made great sacrifices to help defend our freedoms.

QUOTABLE QUOTES

Give me your tired, your poor, your huddled
masses yearning to breathe free.
—*Emma Lazarus,* American poet

O beautiful for spacious skies,
For amber waves of grain,
For purple mountain majesties
Above the fruited plain!
America! America!
God shed his grace on thee
And crown thy good with brotherhood
From sea to shining sea!
—*Katharine Lee Bates,* American poet and educator

Suggested Messages

- Thank you for helping to keep Independence Day a reality.
- Your bravery and sacrifice aren't going unnoticed. Thank you from the bottom of my heart.
- You asked and answered: "What can I do for my country?" You're an inspiration to all of us.
- Thank you for telling us natives what Independence Day means. We're proud to salute you, fellow American.

- A great day for remembering values near and dear.
- May the sun always rise on a free, strong, and robust America.
- Raise Old Glory high, and let her fly free. Thank you for being such an important part of making it so.
- It's a wonderful thing to be able to hold our freedoms close to heart and mind this day.
- May we never forget the price of our way of life.
- It's a great day to be thankful for all our freedoms, and it's also a perfect day to say thank you, [Name], for the sacrifices you have made to keep us free.
- Let's celebrate this day that commemorates our many, many blessings in this country.
- A red, white, and blue 50-state salute to celebrate this great day.
- Let's assemble ourselves together—at our house—for our annual picnic, fireworks watch, and celebration.
- Hoorah, for the red, white, and blue.
- To our true American friends.

Rosh Hashanah (The Jewish New Year)

This is the Jewish religious New Year that commemorates the creation of the world. This holiday occurs the first and second days of the Hebrew month of *Tishrei*, falling on dates between mid-September and mid-October. The traditional greeting for this holiday is "Happy New Year," or in Hebrew, "*Shana tova.*" The ten days following this day are set aside for worship and introspection, and culminate in the Day of Atonement, Yom Kippur.

Rosh Hashanah signals God opening the book of life, and Yom Kippur signifies God sealing the book. Between these days is a very special time of reflection and prayer, called Shabbat Shuva.

Message Etiquette

Think about the traditions of faith, and past holidays and traditions to get you started. If you don't share the Jewish faith with your recipient, keep your message simple and to the point of wishing her a Happy New Year.

QUOTABLE QUOTE

So as we observe the state of the nation and the world, see their progress and their struggle, we can and we should observe the state of our own being. Not only in terms of how much more we are doing, observing, and learning, but also in terms of how much more deeply and sensitively we are living.
—*Rabbi David Lapin,* American spiritual leader and teacher

Suggested Messages

- Happy New Year, and best wishes to our dear friends. You're often in our thoughts.
- Thinking of all of you at this very special time of review, contemplation, and new beginnings.
- We are hoping your New Year will be filled with all sweet, good things.
- To our dear friends of many years, we so look forward to celebrating the New Year with you.

- Wishing you all good things for the New Year.
- Our best wishes for a happy, healthy, and wonderful New Year.
- At the time of reflection, we remember with fondness all the wonderful years of our friendship. Our sincere wishes for a new year filled with sweetness and light.
- *Shana tova* to you and all of yours.
- Many thoughts of past years bring fond remembrances of you.
- We rejoice in your friendship so closely tied with our reflections on the past and hopes for a sweet new year. Our families and lives are tied together.
- Shalom!
- May all your prayers be answered in this wonderful new year.
- Our thoughts and prayers are with you and for you this holy season.
- Our wishes for a great gathering and a week of celebration.
- May the great joy and hopes of this season of celebration be yours.
- May this be a season of renewed faith and new beginnings.
- Our sincere wishes for a fresh start and a new year filled with spiritual wisdom.
- May you be inscribed and sealed; and may you have a healthy new year filled with material and spiritual success!

Christmas

Christmas is the Christian holiday celebrating the birth of Jesus Christ. The word comes from *Cristes maesse,* or "Christ's Mass," which many historians believe began in Rome about A.D. 336, as a result of Constantine the Great, the first Christian Roman emperor, introducing Christmas as an immovable feast to be commemorated on December 25. Some believe he picked this date to combine existing pagan celebrations on or near the date together with observing the birth of Jesus. Early Christians resisted this date for that very reason: it commemorated the pagan festival of the worship of Saturn, or the God of Harvest, and Mithras, the God of Light. At the same time, Northern Europeans celebrated harvest festival, while other cultures celebrated winter solstice on December 22, the shortest day of the year.

But many of the Christmas traditions we have today date back even earlier. In early Mesopotamia, for example, one god, Murduk, of the many worshipped, was celebrated in a 12-day festival called Zagmuth. This is where the 12 days of Christmas are believed to have originated. Ancient Romans decorated their homes with garlands and trees lit with candles in celebration of their god Saturn. Feasting and entertaining was part of the celebration, as was the giving of gifts. The burning of the yuletide log started as part of a Scandinavian solstice celebration called Yuletide.

Around A.D. 350, the Bishop of Rome, Pope Julius I, declared December 25 as the annual day to observe Christmas. But the early Romans couldn't practice their faith openly, so there was little celebration until Christianity became the official religion of the Roman Empire at the end of that century.

Although other cultures had observed Christmas on dates varying from January to May, by the fifth century A.D., December 25 had become the accepted date throughout the world.

Some of the other traditions of Christmas adopted over the centuries include St. Nicholas, or as he has become known, Santa Claus (from the Dutch *Sinterklaas*), who was a Christian leader from Smyrna (today's Turkey) in the fourth century. St. Nicholas wanted to give to the poor anonymously. So, he climbed onto a rooftop and dropped a bag of money down the chimney. It landed in a girl's stocking put by the fire to dry. This may explain today's tradition of Santa coming down the chimney. And also stockings hung by the fire.

It took centuries for the celebration of Christmas to blossom. Oliver Cromwell, for example, banned Christmas festivities in England between 1649 and 1660. But with the settlement of the colonies in the United States, joyous celebrations of Christmas began to take hold.

Christmas celebrations became more popular in the 19th century. In 1820, Washington Irving's book *The Keeping of Christmas at Bracebridge Hall* helped popularize Christmas; and in 1834, Britain's Queen Victoria brought her German husband, Prince Albert, into Windsor Castle, and introduced from Europe the traditions of the Christmas tree and the singing of Christmas carols.

Sending Christmas greetings is believed to have started with the practice of having English schoolboys write notes of Christmas greetings to their parents. This practice was helped along in 1840 when the first public postal deliveries began. In 1843, Sir Henry Cole, the first director of the Victoria and Albert Museum, created the first greeting card when he commissioned artist John Callcott Horsley to design and illustrate a three-panel card with the message "Merry Christmas and a Happy New Year to You," which he sent to his friends. Printing Christmas cards in large quantities became possible with the advent of a new printing press in about 1860. Still, it wasn't until 1870 that Ulysses S. Grant declared Christmas a national holiday in the United States.

Message Etiquette

Today, in the United States, the common phrase for Christmas greetings is "Merry Christmas"; in the United Kingdom and Canada, it's "Happy Christmas." Often, greetings for Christmas are combined with wishes for the New Year and sent in a single greeting card. In this case, the greetings are combined: "Merry Christmas and Happy New Year."

Personalize your message to the recipient with a few lines of personal greeting and your handwritten signature(s). You might start by thinking of a shared memory of another Christmas season, or a point of shared celebration of the season.

As for sending greeting cards by email, a good rule is that for people you know primarily by email—and actively exchange emails with—an electronic greeting is acceptable. But it doesn't have the personal touch and demonstrated care of a handwritten and mailed greeting. So, to keep the long tradition of sending handwritten messages to friends and relatives during the holiday season, invest the love, time, and effort to create and mail a special season's greeting.

QUOTABLE QUOTES

She will bear a Son; and you shall call His name Jesus,
for He will save His people from their sins.
—Bible. Matthew 1:21

For unto you is born this day in the city of David
a Savior, which is Christ the Lord.
—*Bible. Luke 2:11*

Suggested Messages

- From the [Name]s to the [Name]s, special wishes for a blessed Christmas.
- You are a very important part of our Christmas celebrations; and we look forward to getting together with you on the 17th.
- Christmas traditions are an important part of binding us together. We wish you a blessed Christmas season.
- In celebration of the birthday of our Lord, we reach across the miles with this huge Christmas hug!
- It's a very special time to renew old friendships and catch up on all the events of this year. (We're waiting for your annual Christmas letter to learn what the [Name] family has been up to.) We wish you all a very blessed Christmas season that lasts the whole year through.
- May the light of this season burn brightly in your hearts.
- Although we don't share the same religious beliefs, there is a strong bond of friendship and care between us. And we want to wish you a very rich and meaningful celebration.
- Merry, merry Christmas, and a very Happy New Year.
- We hope to share the joy of this season with you in the coming weeks.
- I never sing "Deck the Halls" without thinking how lovely your home looks at this time of year with all the painstakingly placed decorations. Special wishes for a wonderful—and fully decked-out—Christmas season.

- Peace to you all, and joy in abundance during this holy season. May it spread the whole world around.
- Light and life, peace and joy to you all.
- It's true: this is truly the most wonderful time of the year. Our greetings and best wishes for a rich and rewarding Christmas to the [Name]s.
- God bless all in the household of the [Name]s, as we pray for peace in our world and joy and rejoicing in all our hearts.
- Peace on earth, and to your family in full measure.
- May the bright miracle of Christmas live in your hearts.
- How we look forward to celebrating this season with you. Wishing you a happy and safe journey home for Christmas.
- May the spirit of this holy season bring its very special joy and peace to all the [Name]s.
- Health, happiness, peace, and joy to all of you [Name]s.
- May the love and light of the season illuminate your hearts and home.
- Our best wishes for a blessed Christmas that brings all the [Name]s together from far and wide.
- Joy, peace, and happiness for this Christmas season.
- It's the season of giving and joy, and you always come to mind in those categories, [Name].
- Joy in abundance for Christmas, and health and happiness for the New Year.
- A very, very Merry Christmas to all of you.
- The warmest of wishes for a season filled to overflowing with good things.
- Wishes from our house to yours for all things bright and beautiful for the Christmas season.

- Best wishes for a lightness and glow throughout your celebrations.
- Love and blessings to you in full and abundant measure.
- Joy to the world of [Name]s. And peace on earth and in each of your hearts.

Hanukkah
(The Jewish Festival of Lights)

The word for this holy Jewish holiday, Hanukkah, means dedication. The holiday commemorates the rededication of the Temple in Jerusalem after its 165 B.C.E. recapture by the Maccabees from the Hellenist Syrians, who had seized it in 168 B.C.E., and had dedicated it to the worship of Zeus.

The fighting began in Modiin, a village not far from Jerusalem, after Mattathias, a Jewish High Priest, refused to take part in a Syrian pagan ceremony. After the recapture of the Temple, Judah Maccabee and his soldiers wanted to relight the golden menorah in the Temple, but found only a day's worth of oil. Miraculously, the oil lasted for eight days, which gave them time to obtain a new supply.

Today the celebration of Hanukkah includes lighting one candle in a menorah each night to commemorate this eight-day miracle. The holiday is also called the Festival of Lights. It lasts for eight days (and eight nights) starting on the 25th day of Kislev on the Hebrew calendar, sometime between the end of November to the middle of December.

Today celebrations are rich with traditional foods and the giving of a gift for each day of the celebration.

Message Etiquette

You may wish to send Jewish families and friends you hold near and dear personal greetings at this holiday time. Those who don't share the Jewish faith may send a very simple greeting of best wishes for a blessed and joyous Hanukkah season, or holiday.

Focus first on the person to whom you are sending the greeting, then on the celebration and dedication. It's also appropriate to recount the family traditions of this very special time of year, or memories from Hanukkahs past.

QUOTABLE QUOTES

Kindle the taper like the steadfast star
Ablaze on evening's forehead o'er the earth,
And add each night a lustre till afar
An eightfold splendor shine above thy hearth.
—*Emma Lazarus,* American poet

Colorful candles burning bright,
each lit on eight very special nights.
—*Anonymous*

May the lights of Hanukkah usher
in a better world for all humankind.
—*Anonymous*

Suggested Messages

- Happy Hanukkah to you.
- May the light of this holiday season shine brightly in all your hearts, [Name]s.
- Best wishes as you celebrate the miracles of this season.
- We're sending you our happy Hanukkah wishes for the holiday.
- A bright and happy Hanukkah to you and all your family.
- May the celebration of traditions this Hanukkah draw all your hearts close together.
- I hold as very, very precious all my memories of Hanukkah and the times spent with you. Happy Hanukkah.
- May the traditions of this season warm your hearts and bring all your family together this Hanukkah.
- Remembering the Hanukkah celebrations we've shared, and our times together at this time of year is precious, indeed.
- Happy are the memories of Hanukkah with you. Our best wishes for this blessed season, till we see you.
- Our wishes for a very special and blessed Hanukkah.
- May the rejoicing and blessings of the Hanukkah season be yours.
- Some of my happiest, and most meaningful, memories of childhood are of Hanukkah, observing the traditions of so many generations. Thank you for your important role in creating those memories.
- We hold you near and dear at this wonderful time of celebration.

- You are in our hearts and on our minds this Hanukkah as we light the candles and remember our rich heritage. Happy Hanukkah season to all of you.
- Love, peace, and light in all your hearts this Hanukkah season.
- Eight days of blessings to you, and many more, as you light the candles this Hanukkah season.
- May all the riches of the traditions of this season and our cherished memories of family celebrations embrace you this season.
- Best wishes for this very special season.
- Thank you, [Name], for all the precious experiences of celebrating Hanukkahs past together. Each will live in my heart forever, and I will pass them on to my children and grandchildren, as you have to me.
- We're missing your presence this very special season, but our sincere hopes and prayers for a very special Hanukkah season at your house.
- Lighting of the candles reminds us of the rich traditions of this season, and also of all those special times of family celebrations. We cherish them all, and hold you close to our hearts.
- Happy Hanukkah wishes to all in the [Name] family.

Kwanzaa

Established in 1966, Kwanzaa was created to connect African Americans to their African roots, and to celebrate the seven Swahili values of family, community, and culture: unity, self-determination, collective work and responsibility, cooperative economics, purpose, creativity, and faith. It's celebrated from December 26 to January 1 each year, with one day set aside to focus on one of these seven values.

Message Etiquette

Personal greetings for Kwanzaa are best focused on points of shared history, community unity, and present connections. It's always proper to tell people how special they are, and what they mean to you.

Start by thinking of the person's individual virtues that personally express aspects of their self-determination, unity, community spirit, collective work, cooperative interdependence, purpose, creativity, and faith. Use memories or hopes for starting your thoughts, and mention how the community has, or can, benefit from the person's future contributions.

QUOTABLE QUOTES

The moment we break faith with one another,
the sea engulfs us and the light goes out.
—*James Baldwin,* American author

No man is an island, entire of itself;
every man is a piece of the continent.
—*John Donne,* English poet

Remember upon the conduct of each
depends the fate of all.
—*Alexander the Great,* King of Macedonia

In union there is strength.

—*Aesop*, Greek storyteller

So powerful is the light of unity
that it can illuminate the whole earth.

—*Baháʼuʼlláh*, Founder of the Baháʼi faith

In all things that are purely social we can be as separate
as the fingers, yet one as the hand in all things
essential to mutual progress.

—*Booker T. Washington*, American educator and author

Suggested Messages

- [Name], leading the community drive for creating the community center last year demonstrated all the principles of Kwanzaa. You've helped so many to learn the secret of community spirit.
- We loved working with you on the community garden, and look forward to celebrating with you at dinner on Thursday. Happy Kwanzaa.
- What a wonderful job you did on the Klub Kids. It's a real reason to celebrate this Kwanzaa season.
- Best wishes to you, [Name], for the harvest we'll enjoy over the Kwanzaa season that will symbolize a surplus from our souls. We look forward to sitting around the table with you in this great time of celebration.
- For the wonderful heritage we share, the traditions that are ours, and all our hopes for our community of brothers and sisters in the future, we send wishes for a rewarding and expressive Kwanzaa season.

- It's a great time to look back with love, and look forward with hope in our hearts. We celebrate with you for all the community projects that have been planned and executed. And we look forward to sharing many more dreams during this season. Best wishes for new successes.
- To our friends who are the embodiment of all things Kwanzaa. We love sharing in your industry, and your heart for the community. A happy, rewarding holiday season to the [Name]s.
- To community, faith, responsibility, cooperation, and unity. And to all the cherished values of Kwanzaa. We look forward to the many worthwhile ideas and projects that will surely be produced in our time together this season.
- Our hearts are filled with the joy of our joint great accomplishments this year. We can hardly wait to hear about all your other successes this past year. Happy holidays.
- We applaud your great determination and contribution to the community school project. We can hardly wait to hear the details at this Kwanzaa celebration, and to discuss next year's project.
- We're looking forward to the lighting of candles and sharing of traditions, pride, accomplishments, and visions for the future.
- May your Kwanzaa be filled with joy, pride, and visions for unity.

PART FOUR

Social Grace Messages

Beyond those simple tenets of etiquette (which are, granted, so often missing in our society)—respect for others, consideration of the rights of others, and honesty— there exists a whole higher realm of spiritual possibilities: connection, love, communion, and shared joy, to name a few. It's to this elevated level of relationships that this section is devoted. It requires writing from a deeper level of yourself that includes both the hand and the heart. And it requires living, and giving, from a generous spirit.

Such generosity can be practiced and cultivated, and it reaps beautiful rewards for both the giver and the recipient.

Thank You

Saying a proper thank-you—practicing gratitude—is one of the essential tenets of civility. It says we value the participation of others in our lives, and their kindness toward us. This isn't a reflexive parroting the word "thanks," or even a more formal "thank-you." It's expressing a spirit of gratitude for something that was given to you. It's been scientifically demonstrated that expressing thanks can make you happier, too, as well as spread your joy, plus a measure, back to the giver. It's a wonderful law of life: multiplying the joy.

Look closely and you find that the act of saying thank you has three essential parts: (1) recognizing a gift or act; (2) acknowledging it; and (3) conveying appreciation for it. And, when you do it from these combined sources—heart and mind—you connect with the giver, and, amazingly, you will also feel the desire to give to others. Saying thanks, or expressing gratitude, can produce a positive, flowing force. And, yes, it can be contagious!

Message Etiquette

Thanking the giver for a gift, a thoughtful deed, or an act of kindness should be done *in kind,* and in a timely fashion. (A quick thank you delivered by email after someone has hosted a party for you that took weeks of planning and preparation, for example, will *not* do. It's boorish. It's rude. It's insulting.)

Start by focusing on the giver, then the gift or act. Connect the gift to the giver; and then connect yourself to the gift or act, and express your thanks. Most often, your card of thanks will not contain a prepared message beyond the printed "Thank You," so just start with the person you're thanking, or the gift.

And be sure to send your thank you within one to three days after receiving the gift or act, unless it was given during a very emotionally charged or demanding period of time, like the death of a relative, a wedding, or a huge theater production.

QUOTABLE QUOTES

If the only prayer you say in life is "thank you,"
it would be enough.
—*Meister Eckhart,* German theologian and philosopher

Silent gratitude isn't much use to anyone.
—*Gladys Bertha Stern,* English author and playwright

To speak gratitude is courteous and pleasant,
to enact gratitude is generous and noble,
but to live gratitude is to touch Heaven.
—*Johannes A. Gaertner,* German-born American poet and author

No duty is more urgent than returning thanks.
—*Saint Ambrose,* Roman bishop

A thankful heart is a happy heart.
—*Anonymous*

When any original act of charity or of gratitude, for
instance, is presented to our sight or imagination, we are
deeply impressed with its beauty and feel a strong desire
in ourselves of doing charitable and grateful acts also.
—*Thomas Jefferson,* American president

If you want to lift yourself up,
lift someone else up.
—*Booker T. Washington,* American educator and author

Suggested Messages—In Steps

You'll want to complete all three of the following steps to express
your thanks, depending on what the gift was, and how it was given:

1. **Start by focusing on the giver.**
   - You are truly the most thoughtful person I know,
     [Name], . . .
   - You added sparkle to my day . . .
   - Your kindness was both a surprise and a delight . . .
   - [Name], what is your secret to selecting the perfect
     gift? . . .
   - You, [Name], are a trendsetter in the gift-giving depart-
     ment . . .
   - Your thoughtfulness and generosity meant so much . . .
   - [Name], you really know how to make a day special . . .

- Wonderful, wonderful you . . .
- [Name], what a kind heart you have . . .
- Your loving kindness shows through in such unique ways . . .
- No one else would have thought of such a terrific gift . . .
- Thank you for being as terrific as always . . .
- A deed well done may well have been done by you, [Name], . . .
- Your strength and support will never be forgotten . . .
- You do superb hospitality! . . .
- Because of your efforts, [Name], . . .

2. Name the gift or kindness.
- Once upon a time there was a wonderful aunt named [Name], who always remembered her niece's birthday with a delightful gift. This year she outdid herself with the gift of [name the gift] . . .
- I really didn't realize how very prescient you are, [Name]; I was on my very last tablespoon of gourmet coffee . . .
- There are great dividends in having the best shopper on the planet for a best friend, as you demonstrated with your gift of a wreath for the holidays . . .
- Who was the cutest flower girl who ever dropped a rose petal at her auntie's wedding? . . .
- Only you could have dreamed up the perfect gift: a spa day! . . .
- Dancing to the Oldies—thought up by the hostess with the powers of perfect party planning and execution . . .
- Your wonderful carrot cake is only surpassed by your generosity . . .

3. Connect yourself, or gratitude and/or relationship to the gift, and your thanks, and add a note of inclusion and future connection or sharing, if possible.

- No one but you, [Name], could have put together a more delightful and perfect party combo of food and frolic. I've never been more surprised—and you know how I <u>love</u> surprises. Everything was perfect, and I (a.k.a. supersleuth) didn't have the slightest inkling a party was in the making. Thank you for (yet another) spectacular <u>29th birthday</u> celebration. You created a very special memory for me, and I was thrilled. I'm going to have to think really, really hard before your birthday comes up in February.

- Your taste is impeccable, as always, [Name]. The red sweater is a perfect match to my paisley skirt. I love it, love it, love it. Thank you for being the best friend a girl ever had. Here's proof positive that you picked exactly the right gift. Don't I look like the best-dressed speaker on the panel? I'll wear it to the luncheon on Thursday, so you can see for yourself.

- You really brightened my day with the delicious chicken soup Tom brought over. One more piece of evidence of your outstanding culinary skills, and your thoughtfulness. I'll always think of your chicken soup as the thing that accounted for my quick recovery and return to work. (A mixed blessing, of course.) Thank you, [Name], for your kindness. I look forward to you coming to dinner on Friday for my very pedestrian pot roast.

- Being locked out of my house was never so much fun.

What a golden neighbor you are to take in a woman with only a briefcase and a big appetite. Thank you for the sandwich, the laughter, and the use of your lovely guest room. Your kindness and care turned my disaster into delight. I hope this plant will replace that one you've been bidding good-bye.

- Very rare is the woman who makes guests feel completely at ease and at home during such a difficult time. You are a gem, indeed, [Name]. Thank you for your generous and warm heart. We so appreciate your acts of kindness, and look forward to seeing you next week.

- Walking Scruffy after my ankle sprain was so kind of you, [Name]; but, of course, we knew you were a truly wonderful neighbor. We just didn't know how wonderful. Thank you from the bottom of my heart. I simply couldn't have kept Scruffy at home after my injury if it hadn't been for your help. And please tell Miss Kitty Fluff this little gift is for all those mornings she had to endure watching from her window seat as you walked a dog. That had to rank at the very top of the feline humiliations chart.

- I'm now the proud owner of eight perfectly matched mugs that add the kind of pizzazz to my kitchen it's been missing in the "comfy, let's have a cup of coffee" department. Who knew that all our coffee hour needed was this designer's touch? Not I. You're a master, [Name]. I'm thrilled with them. And now, of course, we'll have to do coffee every Friday morning—my house, my new [Name] mugs! Thank you for your exquisite taste and thoughtfulness. See you Friday at 10:00 A.M.?

- Only you could have dreamed up the perfect gift: a spa

day! A deep and loving thank you from your (formerly) Twisted Sister! I'm trying to think of a proper way to reciprocate.

- Who knew that what I needed in my office to be more productive was a mister? My very brilliant colleague, and perfect gift-buyer, [Name], that's who. I believe my production is up 23% since the mister was installed. (That has yet to be reflected in my salary, of course. But I'm working on that, too.) Thank you, thank you, thank you. Even my newly lush and green-leafed plants thank you.

- I have long known of your great powers and influence, but taking 10 years off my hips? Now that's something I never would have believed was on your resume. But you did it with the smashing new slacks you gave me. (And without the pain of commitment to an exercise program, which would never have happened.) I'm totally delighted. I even got a "Wow" from [Name]! I'm looking forward to that ball game when you can see for yourself.

Appreciation

One of the most delightful aspects of sending a greeting card with your personal note of appreciation is that the recipient isn't expecting it. You're initiating the message because it's something you want to do, something you want to express.

Expressing gratitude and appreciation, it turns out, has benefits to both the recipient of your message, and to you, the message writer. Experiments done at the University of Pennsylvania in Professor Martin Seligman's positive psychology laboratories indicated that those who wrote gratitude letters to people who'd been especially kind to them, or who made significant positive differences, then read the letters to the persons they appreciated, experienced more happiness and less depression than they had before the experiment. Amazing.

It may be difficult to find exactly the *right* greeting card you want to express exactly the respect and adulation you want to someone who has performed her job in an extraordinary way, gone beyond the expected duties of her role, offered support over time, or otherwise created in you the desire to tell her how much you appreciate what she has done. If you can't find what you want, send a personal message on your own note card or stationery.

Message Etiquette

The key to writing your note is heartfelt sincerity. The central point is that you've taken notice of something the person has done, or a value she has exhibited, and you appreciate it. So, you will, of course, focus on the person and her act. Maybe it's something as routine as the fact that Sally, who carpools with you to get the kids to school, is always on time and completely dependable. That's praiseworthy. You can count on her; and you do. Maybe it's the manager of the apartment building or condo association where you live, who always keeps the mail area clean and uncluttered. Or, maybe it's a firefighter who is dedicated to keeping your community, or another, safe. Or, a heroic policeman. Or, even the young guy in the office mailroom, who goes out of his way to do his job carefully.

It's satisfying and rewarding for the recipient of your message to learn that you recognize that she has done her job well, and that you appreciate her and her efforts. And you have the power to communicate that to someone in your life. Make it a practice when you are aware of extraordinary effort, a job done in an exemplary fashion, or excellence in the line of duty. You may find it addictive, and an added reward of practicing the principle of appreciation is a happier you, too.

QUOTABLE QUOTES

A man who does not love praise is not a full man.
—*Henry Ward Beecher,* American clergyman and reformer

Plant a tree under which you never plan
to sit and enjoy the shade.
—*Anonymous*

The applause of a single human being
is of great consequence.
—*Samuel Johnson,* English author

Suggested Messages

- Just because my flower beds look anemic and neglected doesn't mean I don't enjoy beautiful flowers. I do. And each spring I'm so delighted to look across the street and see your masterfully manicured flower beds in full bloom. Your efforts are enjoyed and appreciated by the whole neighborhood.
- I just needed to tell you that I never worry when I see your name on the church usher list for Sunday morning service. I can roll over and take another five minutes, because not once in ten years have I had to call and check with you to make sure you remember your duty.

I just wanted to tell you that I appreciate your dedication and trustworthiness.

- I just wanted to tell you that I <u>so</u> appreciate the volunteer work you do for our school. I know that Dinara and Rox will always have their tutor show up on Tuesdays. And I've watched the improvement in their reading and math skills. You have made a difference in these two young lives. I so appreciate your great work with these students.

- You've made my life run so much smoother, and I just wanted to tell you how much I appreciate being in the carpool with you. I don't know how I got so lucky, but your dependability and thoughtfulness have taken the word "hysteria" out of my afternoon vocabulary. Also, my 7:00 A.M. vocabulary. Now I look forward to Mondays and Thursdays. Your efforts on behalf of our kids are greatly appreciated by this parent.

- Each month at my investment club and book club, I hear terrible mother-in-law tales of slights and insults. But I have nothing to contribute in the complaint department. I just want to say how much I value our relationship. [Name], I so appreciate all your efforts to work at building a wonderful daughter-in-law/mother-in-law relationship. And I look forward to becoming even better friends, as well as truly great in-laws.

- I drive by the firehouse once a week on my way to the grocery store, and each time I'm reminded what an important job you do to keep our community safe. I just wanted to say on behalf of my family that we sleep easily at night knowing you all are there, ready to respond to an emergency.

- Emma is (finally) learning basic math skills that have,

up until now, not made sense to her. At long last, it isn't a daily morning battle to get her to prepare for school. Miss Adams, you've worked a miracle for our family— and certainly for Emma—and from our hearts, Tom and I want to express how we appreciate all you do for your third-grade flock. But especially, of course, we appreciate what you've done for our Emma.

- [Name], before you became manager at our condo building, I would scurry through the hallways and down to the mail area before hosting a dinner party to be sure that things didn't look too neglected. Since you've been on board, I've come to know that we will all be represented well when visitors to the building arrive. The entry is gorgeous with the new plants, the mail area is spotless, and the hallways are sparkling. You are doing a fantastic job, and we appreciate it.

- Through rain, sleet, and snow, [Name], you've faithfully delivered our mail. And you've even put up with the mad terrier, Hurricane, when something has to be received and you're required to ring the bell. We're spoiled. And you've done it with your careful attention to detail and dedication to duty. We appreciate all you do, and do so well.

- I just need to say, [Name], how much I appreciate your volunteering as chapel coordinator. I don't wonder for a single moment whether you'll show up 30 minutes before the service, straighten the hymnals, pick up the clutter, and put on a welcoming smile for all the veterans who come to join us. Please know that you make a difference, a very real difference to so many.

Bon Voyage

Nearly everything is sweeter when it is shared, and that's true, too, of travel. So, expressing that very sentiment when someone you know is taking off on a trip is a great way to extend your good wishes and help to increase the enjoyment of the departing traveler.

Message Etiquette

The French term *bon voyage* (have a good trip), is used to convey our wishes that friends or family enjoy their travel adventure. You may want to couple your good wishes with a wish for a future engagement, or add a note about something you found particularly wonderful on your trip to the same destination.

QUOTABLE QUOTES

Not traveling is like living in the Library of Congress
but never taking out more than one or two books.
—*Marilyn vos Savant,* American author and playwright

May the road rise up to meet you,
May the wind be always at your back . . .
—*Irish proverb*

Wealth I ask not, hope nor love,
Not a friend to know me;
All I ask, the heaven above
And the road below me.
—*Robert Louis Stevenson,* Scottish poet and author

My heart is warm with the friends I make,
And better friends I'll not be knowing;
Yet there isn't a train I wouldn't take,
No matter where it's going.
—*Edna St. Vincent Millay*, American poet and playwright

Suggested Messages

- May the weather be fair, the exchange rate favorable, and the destinations along the way create memories you'll forever hold dear.
- We loved our trip to [destination], and are sure you will, too. Here's what we would have on our don't-miss list if we were going this spring: the small antiques shops along [Name] Avenue, the marketplace at [Name], and the artists along the [Name]. Encounters at these areas rank as some of our best memories.
- I'm enclosing a trip journal for you, and hope you'll find—as I did—that keeping this kind of record allows you, later, to instantly relive a small and wonderful respite back to the glorious places you'll visit. Have a marvelous time!
- Our best wishes go with you as you embark on this wonderful adventure.
- We can hardly wait for the posttrip review. I'll host. Just let me know when, after you return. We'll look forward to one of your marvelous travelogues. Have a wonderful time.
- The best advice I got before taking the trek you're setting out on was: Travel light and embrace everything you encounter. You'll have a delightful time. (You'll want to take your electrical adaptors.)

- I'm mentioning to the sun goddess that you'll be looking for her help on your journey. And we'll be keeping sunny thoughts for you here, too. Have a terrific time.
- Here's wishing you sunny, sunny days, moonlit and star-studded nights, and dancing until dawn. Have a spectacular cruise.
- What a great opportunity to taste the world! Literally. I can't think of a better objective than to eat and drink your way around France.
- You're the best of travelers, and your itinerary looks delicious. Have a wonderful time.
- We'd like to have a very brief "Bon Voyage" get together on Sunday about 7:00 P.M. Just for an hour. Let me know if this will work for you. Yes or no, have a delightful trip.
- When in Rome . . . Have the most wonderful time!
- Our good wishes for golden days, nights under a canopy of brightly lit stars, and a priceless adventure.

Retirement

This time-honored milestone is changing dramatically for many seniors around the globe. What once meant a matriculation from a lifelong career of employment with a single organization to a new "retiree" status to pursue a life of leisure, may now be a transition from one type of career endeavor to another. Or, for many, there will be no phase of life that's called "retirement" at all. For others, it may arrive only after a number of postponements.

In these times, it's very important that you know the exact circumstances, and the just-minted retiree's outlook on her new state of leisure or new occupation before writing your message.

Message Etiquette

If you focus on the person to whom you're directing your message and tune in to how she feels about her new status, you'll be able to hit exactly the right note.

Time your message to arrive with the event, or very shortly thereafter. You may want to include an invitation to get together and celebrate with lunch, a round of golf, tennis, or dinner; or something that indicates a continuing relationship. Or, you may want to plan an all-out retirement bash.

You may also want to send a second message to the retiree after she's had a few months in her new role. (Again, tune in first. People achieve comfort in this new status at very different rates, times, and measures.)

QUOTABLE QUOTES

So now it's twice as much husband
and half as much income?
—*Anonymous*

Few men of action have been able to make
a graceful exit at the appropriate time.
—*Malcolm Muggeridge,* English writer and social critic

Suggested Messages

- Retire? I don't think so. Knowing you, I'd call it a new beginning, and I'm going to be betting on a brand-new career for you, too, [Name].

- [Name], you personify innovation, and I'm looking forward to seeing what, exactly, you bring to the vocation of retired. I'm sure it will be revolutionary and patentable.
- No pressure, but we expect you'll be wildly euphoric and superbly skilled at your new position: retired.
- So, will it be the golf pro tour, or the club tennis doubles ladder? Whatever you put your mind and hand to in this new phase of your life, we have every confidence you'll excel at it. All our best wishes.
- Best wishes for a spectacular new adventure. You'll make a real success of it, we're sure.
- I'm sure that Monday morning, [Date], will find you hard at work on the [project name] in your workshop. Look out [competition name], here he comes!
- Fly-fishing, backpacking, kayaking, and triathlons. I can see your future clearly, and it all looks wonderful. Happy adventures to you, [Name].
- There aren't many people transitioning into your phase of life I'd like to emulate. But you are one. Such creativity and panache. Where will you apply yourself? I'm betting on that novel.
- I know we'll be seeing your name up in lights again: "Volunteer of the Year"; "New Big Mouth Bass Competition Winner"; or "Symphony Names Most Valuable New Member." You'll distinguish yourself in your new chosen endeavor, just as you have with everything else you've decided to take on. It'll be delightful to see! Congratulations.
- Now the world will hold endless possibilities! Congratulations, [Name]. I'm sure you won't waste a minute of it.

- Late nights, late mornings, and open schedules. Who wouldn't love the potential these indulgences pose? Best wishes for your new world of everything's-possible dreams.
- Here's to brand-new beginnings, and the best years of your life!
- All things are possible for you now, [Name]. Best wishes for golden days ahead.
- All life's abundance is what we're wishing for you in life's "new lane."
- It's a grand thing when you get to call all the shots, and then carry out the plan of action. You'll do it with great form. Oh, and you'll still be taking out the garbage, too, I'm guessing.
- Retirement is just another word for fantastic, constant vacation, and days in the sun (or shade). You'll get the hang of it by Thursday when we have a 10:00 A.M. tee time. Congratulations!
- I suppose this means I'll no longer hold the top spot on the tennis ladder. With all that additional practice time, your forehand will become even more deadly. Ah, well, it's been a good run for me. Bring it on, Champ.
- How, exactly, does one so fit and young get to become a person of leisure? However you managed it, you'll make a great success of it.
- Our heartfelt thoughts and wishes for all things wonderful in your future.
- Poker, gardening, pinochle, and canasta. There's no stopping you now. Best wishes for a super retirement.
- It's a brand-new beginning, a wonderful new challenge. Now, you get to make all your own rules. And you'll

be your own boss and write your own performance reviews—well, except for [Spouse Name]'s. Here's to your happy new life!

- All your hard work has paid off; the life of your dreams awaits you. Best wishes.

- May all your tulips and columbines come up golden (except for the lavender ones).

- You have been indispensable to [Company Name], and we applaud all you accomplished here. We will all miss you greatly. But we know there's a very large sailfish waiting for you in Costa Rica. Happy retirement.

- Best wishes for smooth and happy sailing ahead, [Name].

Friendship and Family

Friendships—like all living organisms—need nurturing. And that goes double for building and growing close and harmonious relationships with family members. Keeping these relationships well, healthy, and vibrant can be supplemented with a regular diet of personal handwritten messages on greeting cards, as well as on your own personal stationery. This is a very special vehicle you may use for bond building. Sure, the telephone is a wonderful tool and long-distance rates have diminished or disappeared for many of us, and email is great, too; but there's nothing that can substitute for finding that special hand-addressed envelope or package in the mailbox with a personal message written by the hand of someone close. It's a wonderful way to keep the lifeblood flowing between you and friends and relatives.

You may develop the habit of enclosing things of interest,

too, like canceled stamps you know your friend needs for her collection, a recipe you're sure she'll love, a photo for her photo album, small mementos and items you find while shopping that you know she'll appreciate. Two friends have maintained the practice of surprising each other with a gift box of very special treats, delivered at carefully orchestrated times, such as when one comes over the finish line after an extreme sports event. The box may contain a bar of favorite bath soap, a wonderful shampoo, a special tea, and new socks. Maybe even a small tube of a favorite, scented lotion.

And it goes triple or quadruple in times when your friend or family member is experiencing a period of high emotion—happy, stressful, or sad. Maybe she just had a baby, and is ecstatic; but she's also finding the sleep deprivation and anxiety really difficult to deal with. Or, perhaps she has a new job that is proving more challenging than she'd expected; or, there could be a cautionary health diagnosis and hospitalization with treatments that stretch out into her uncertain future. Nothing says, "I'm here. I get it. I care. You can count on me," like a personal note with a warm, encouraging message.

But, of course, it all depends upon your message, doesn't it?

Message Etiquette

A bit of positive self-talk before you start can put energy, an upbeat tone, and even a bit of joy into your mood. Then you'll be ready to start your message on an upbeat note—even if all your news isn't.

Building strong bonds can best be done through sharing ideas you can explore in written dialogue: planning, anticipating, or reminiscing about experiences you'll share, or have shared; expressing the care and commitment you have for your friend. You'll want to include these expressions in your message.

Close with words of encouragement, an expression of affection, and something that anticipates a relationship in the future.

Building relationships requires a repeated rhythm, like a heartbeat. So, plan to make writing personal notes something you do regularly. You'll find a real personal benefit, too. The act of writing things down allows you to explore and learn what you feel. It gets you in touch with your inner self.

QUOTABLE QUOTES

It is easy to perform a good action, but not easy
to acquire a settled habit of performing such actions.
—*Aristotle,* Greek philosopher and educator

Friendship needs a certain parallelism of life,
a community of thought, a rivalry of aim.
—*Henry Adams,* American author and historian

Friendship is a single soul dwelling in two bodies.
—*Aristotle,* Greek philosopher and educator

All who joy would win
Must share it—happiness was born a twin.
—*Lord Byron,* English poet

A word aptly spoken is like apples of gold
in settings of silver.
—*Bible. Proverbs 25:11*

Friendship is a strong and habitual inclination
in two persons to promote the good
and happiness of one another.
—*Eustace Budgell,* English author

Every man passes his life in the search after friendship.
—*Ralph Waldo Emerson,* American essayist and poet

Have friends. 'Tis a second existence.
—*Baltasar Gracian,* Spanish priest and author

There was nothing I did not discuss with John.
Because we were both writers and both worked
at home our days were filled with the sound
of each other's voices. I did not always think he was right
nor did he always think I was right but we were
each the person the other trusted.
—*Joan Didion,* American author

Suggested Messages

- Here's the recipe for Hot Crabbies—in Grammy's own penmanship—for your copy of our <u>Family Favorites Cookbook.</u> It was always one of David's top ten. I particularly like to use it when I want to create several hot appetizers because it's easy and can be done ahead.
- I'm sure you are meeting your goal of two pounds lost this week. Way to go, [Name]! I found yesterday that a mid-afternoon snack of carrots and celery, which I keep cleaned and ready to eat in a glass of water in the refrigerator, allows me to overcome those midafternoon munchies. You're doing great, [Name], and I can hardly

wait till Monday's weigh-in. I'm enclosing the magnet with our "after" picture on it for your refrigerator. Don't we look svelte and stunning?

- I've attached my thoughts on the copy of the outline indicating what I think works for the teens class. What do you think? Give me your thoughts, please. You can write your comments on the copy next to mine and send it back. I need your input, [Name].

- Here's my new poem. You know how I value your input. I know you'll ponder it before you comment; an investment I'm sure the casual reader won't give me. So, don't be too kind to the poet! Go ahead and write on the copy, and send it back.

- I was delighted when I received the enclosed state postage stamps on letters this week. I know you only needed these states to complete your collection. What's on your "looking for" list now?

- [Name], here are the coupons for the butterfly pavilion for the girls. Let's do the zoo on the 15th, OK?

- Here are the instructions for knitting that sweater you so admired. I adapted the pattern of a much-loved childhood sweater Mom knitted for me. (Do you remember the blue cardigan from fifth grade?) You saw how this sweater fits me. I think you'll be happy with the size of the pattern. It'll look terrific on you, especially in that gorgeous yarn you picked out.

- Here are the health-club passes for our workout sessions, just in case you arrive before I do on Thursday. Hey, I'm looking forward to sculpting more shapely upper arms and getting rid of the Jell-O move from my behind!

I know together we'll both get to our slim and toned goals.

- Triathlon training on Monday, Tuesday, and Thursday. I'm all over it. I'm there. Here's the schedule with the progressions we need to meet to be ready for August 7. I've got mine posted on my bulletin board.

- Here are the dried dahlia seeds from my blue-ribbon winners. It will be delightful to know we both have blooms from the same batch of seeds. Do send me pictures at various stages of growth, and we can compare.

- Who knew we'd become such good friends when we met each other at our boys' Little League game? Neither of us. Here's that picture of the living room cocktail table I love. Does it look like what you saw in the antiques shop? You know how I value your expert interior-decorating opinion. What do you think: will it work in my living room?

- I love doing these written book reviews with you. And, you're right, his descriptions are delicious: a wonderful balance of sparse and complete telling. On page 95, in the first paragraph of <u>Out Stealing Horses,</u> I love Petterson's phrasing, ". . . what my father said and how things really were, were not necessarily the same, and that made the world liquid and hard to hold on to." What are some of your favorites?

Just a Note; Thinking About You; To Cheer You

When an event or memory brings to mind someone you know, it's a great idea to act on your impulse to get in touch. Those impulses come to us in this universe, and it's important to have our antennas up and tuned in. And then to act on them. A "Just a Note," or a "Thinking about You," message is like a tap on the shoulder, with your message saying, "By the way, don't forget that you're an important person in my life," "I haven't forgotten you. You're important to me and others," "You're not alone; I'm here, and I care," and/or "Let's not lose track of each other, what we have together is too important."

Keeping a supply of "Thinking about You," "Just a Note," and "To Cheer You" greeting cards, or your own personal note cards, easily accessible will enable you to just take a few minutes to write down a few lines and send your missive off. Your message has the power to brighten the recipient's day, or to initiate a reconnection between the two of you. It may usher in a few minutes of creative reflection for your recipient—and for you—or buoy her up with a treasured memory. Aren't those all reasons enough to do it?

Message Etiquette

An act of thoughtfulness is always good manners, and when your motive is to cheer or brighten someone's day, or to reconnect, sowing the seeds of kindness will produce the blooming friendship you intend. You may want to send a short message to the friend who's feeling lonely because her only daughter has gone off to college; the new Mom who's feeling housebound and slightly overwhelmed by it all; the colleague who didn't get that promotion, and remains depressed about it; or the friend who has plateaued in her rehab program and is discouraged. Write out those few warm sentences of encouragement and cheer.

QUOTABLE QUOTES

Our life is what our thoughts make it.
—*Marcus Aurelius,* Roman emperor

Great thoughts come from the heart.
—*Marquis de Vauvenargues,* French philosopher

Happiness is the meaning and the purpose of life,
the whole aim and end of human existence
—*Aristotle,* Greek philosopher and educator

Mental reflection is so much more interesting than TV
it's a shame more people don't switch over to it.
—*Robert M. Pirsig,* American author

In the life of one man, never
The same time returns.
—*T. S. Eliot,* American poet and author

Suggested Messages

• You just came to mind while I was gardening. A memory of your lovely garden-club luncheon with all your roses in bloom made me smile with delight. Yours are some of the loveliest roses I've ever seen. I know you'll be back out there again very soon, fertilizing and pruning. I'm hoping that fond memories of all those wonderful blooms you teased into glorious beauties will cheer you until then.

- Just a quick note to say I'm thinking about you and the new baby. I know the sleepless nights of these first months can muffle the joy of new motherhood. Please remember my offer to walk the baby Monday, Wednesday, and Friday at 3:00 P.M. I'd love to.

- We're just putting together the cast for *Westward Ho,* and, of course, I thought of you and your wonderful job last year. Guess who's directing this year? [Name], that's who! Knew you'd love to know.

- Yes, I miss you when you're gone! Memories of our Friday coffee chats occur at least once a week. And that's on the low-estimate side. When will you be coming back for a visit?

- [Name], I'm taking on the job of Junior League Christmas Show committee chair that you so skillfully handled last year. Your name comes up often in our meetings; you set a very high bar for me! But you also set up some great organizational systems that are making my job oh-so-much easier than yours was, I'm sure. Now if I can just step into those giant-sized tracks you left . . .

- Wow, do we miss you in this neighborhood! Every time I exit my garage and see [Name]'s house—which now isn't—across the street, I'm reminded of our great neighborhood get-togethers. Especially the day we had to form a posse to hunt down [Pet's Name], and then three hours later found her locked in the laundry chute!

- Remember the day Chris closed his finger in the door, and you drove us to the emergency room? That screaming baby just turned 10 years old, and has a working index finger, thanks to you. I hope your current neighbors appreciate the wonderful person you are.

- Just a note to say I'm thinking of you, and to send positive thoughts as you go to that interview.

- I'll be thinking about you at 11:00 A.M. tomorrow, when you take those exams. I'm sure you'll ace both of them.

- You were there for me during a very dark time in my life; I can't think of what might have happened if you had not been. Please know I'm here for you during this trying time in your life. You're in my thoughts and prayers each day. Call me anytime, for anything.

- Sometimes I have a thought I know is a value we share. I miss you, and often think about you.

- Every morning when the sun peeks over the hill to the east and I'm sitting on the deck with a cup of coffee, I think of you and our many morning sunrise walks, followed by coffee and deck chats. There's a vacancy in my life where those chats used to live. Perhaps someday again; I miss you.

- We went on one of those winter sleigh rides, and, of course, I thought of you and those we shared during our winters growing up. You come up regularly in my thoughts. We need to talk. Here's my phone number. Please get in touch.

- I didn't think when you left that three months was going to be a very long span of time without you. Well, I was very, very wrong! I miss you, and I'll be delighted when you get home.
- I'm thinking of you today. I know this would have been your 50th wedding anniversary. You're in my thoughts and prayers.
- The Press Club isn't the same without you. I think of you and all your contributions to the club each month. Won't you reconsider? You're simply too valuable a member for us to let go.

Love Notes (and Letters)

Love messages have been written and cherished since the beginning of recorded time. And you should definitely add yours to the annals.

It's an old-fashioned idea in these cyber times, but it's still true: the perfect expression of love can best be found in the reflective art of writing your personal message on a greeting card or on fine-textured stationery, or even on a note card. It will carry your message to the one you love in tangible form.

Message Etiquette

The trickiest part of writing your message of love is *not* taking the measure of your own emotion and spilling it across the page in delicious, poetic prose. No, the trickiest part is first properly measuring the receptivity of your (newly?) intended, and then tuning your message perfectly to that pitch so it will be well received.

For the new romance, a lighter hand and lighter prose is the best approach. Open with a warm but simple greeting; introduce an idea, or recount a memory of time together. Maybe you'll want to briefly tell a story of what you've been doing, or relate how you think or feel about an idea the two of you have discussed. Something unique and personal you share. You may want to use humor if you can do it in a transparently self-deprecating manner.

For two hearts that have declared their love for one another, writing a love message becomes easier, yet more difficult: easier, because you are more assured of the love of your intended; more difficult, because expressing your love requires that you go to a deeper emotional level. And use a richer vocabulary. Let your emotions fly free. But isn't that what this adventure called love is all about? You're up to it, and you'll do just fine.

After your opening, focus on your intended. And get personal. This is where you'll want to name a character attribute, what you admire about it, and even give a personal example from your experience together. Expound upon and explore your intended's ideas, goals, and values.

Your closing should sing with future possibilities and anticipation.

Now, open your heart and let your love pour out through your pen.

QUOTABLE QUOTES

All my soul follows you, love—encircles you—
and I live in being yours.
—*Robert Browning,* English poet

Love is a spirit all compact of fire.
—*William Shakespeare,* English dramatist and poet

Love is an endless mystery.
—*Rabindranath Tagore,*
Indian religious leader, poet, and author

To get the full value of joy
You must have someone to divide it with.
—*Mark Twain,* American humorist and writer

Other men said they have seen angels,
But I have seen thee
And thou art enough.
—*G. E. Moore,* English philosopher

We are most alive when we are in love.
—*John Updike,* American author

The loving are the daring.
—*Bayard Taylor,* American author and playwright

'Tis better to have loved and lost
Than never to have loved at all.
—*Alfred, Lord Tennyson,* English poet

There is no remedy for love but to love more.
—*Henry David Thoreau,* American poet

Many waters cannot quench love,
neither can floods drown it.
—*Bible. Song of Solomon 8:7*

Love is the bright foreigner, the foreign self.
—*Ralph Waldo Emerson,* American essayist and poet

Love we give away is the only love we keep.
—*Elbert Hubbard,* American philosopher and author

If I could write the beauty of your eyes and
in fresh numbers number all your graces . . .
—*William Shakespeare,* English dramatist and poet

Suggested Messages

- Yes, I'll say it, I must: I'm smitten with you. Totally.
- If only you hadn't looked at me with those beguiling eyes, maybe I could have survived your charm and beauty. But not after one fleeting look from those brilliant spheres of azure. I was immediately pierced through the heart. I can't improve on Longfellow: "O lovely eyes of azure / Clear as the waters of a brook that run / Limpid and laughing in the summer sun."
- I knew I loved you the moment I first saw you. Maybe I loved you even before that. What do you think?
- Certainly Shakespeare had you in mind when he wrote, "Shall I compare thee to a summer's day? Thou art more lovely and more temperate." I'd have used "you," but I'll go along with the rest of it.
- My heart belongs to you, Love. You've stolen it forever.
- I guess you know I'm ruined for any other love. I can love you, only you. You're perfect.
- Writing it down on paper doesn't make it any more real, but it does give my love for you a record. I love writing it down, and visualizing you reading it.
- Who said parting is such sweet sorrow? I'm miserable without you. You are my bright and shining star.

- You are poetry to my senses. So sweet a melody, such a perfect pitch.
- I didn't think I'd ever find you: a soul mate, so sweet; a lover, so passionate; and a best friend to love.
- I wasn't looking for love. But then I found you.
- Roses are red, violets are blue. What more can be said? I'm head over heels in love with you. (Yes, and I promise to leave the poetry to the poets in the future.)
- How do I love you? It will take the rest of our lives for me to cover that topic adequately.
- You're the stereo in my heart; the technicolor, too. You're my surround sound, and virtual and real-time reality. I love you.
- Please explain to me how, after just one meeting, I could feel this way? I'm pretty obtuse. It's going to take some time; in fact, lots of time.
- You've amped up the wattage in my life. I now realize my battery was completely dead. I'm completely zapped by you. (But in a thrilling and very good way.)
- Could we be serious for one moment? You've completely unnerved me! I'm a basket case at the mere sight of you.
- This card says it all, but let me just add: I love you with all my heart, [Name].
- It's not too soon to say it: When may I see you again?
- I adore you. I mean I adore who you are, and what you are.
- Talking to you, being with you, having you near—it's the best use of my time I could ever imagine.
- OK, let's just assume that my heart beats an extra beat when I hear your name. Well, sometimes it skips a beat,

too. And, OK, it races when I see you. Let's further assume that my tongue instantly becomes a slab of wood in my mouth—unable to move—and I grin a 5,000-watt grin like an imbecile. What's the matter with me? What's the cure? Please tell me.

- I can't sleep for thinking about you. I can't think without thinking about you.
- I could say that I love your mind, and it's true. But the larger truth is that I'm beginning to feel the same way about the rest of you, as well.
- I hope you're happy. You've completely ruined my contented solitude and erased the joy of my former reclusive life. Now I feel incomplete without you. Drat!
- I'm giving up to the joy of you!
- There's no other quite like you; certainly not for me!
- It's true, you make my happiness complete.
- Yes, even my very dreams are yours!
- How could I ever have thought I cared for anyone else, even a tiny bit?
- I can't get that wonderful afternoon out of my head. The perfect picnic, the wind, the sky. And you! Now that I reflect upon it, you're what made it all so perfect.
- I have never—not even once—been called a romantic. And now I am, because of you. You are the romance in my romantic.
- What happens when you stir sugar into a hot cup of tea? Where does one end, the other begin? There is no beginning of one, or end of the other. It's a perfect fusion. That's what your love has done to my life.
- Drugged and dreamy, and completely happy. That's how I feel with you.

- I'm not touching earth this week, not since our dinner on Thursday.
- I no longer doubt the stars in the sky, or the moon lying comfortably on its back. There's no reason to doubt my love for you, darling.
- Yes, you had to go. But why did you have to take the sun, the moon, the stars, and the gentle breezes with you? Please return quickly before I suffocate without you.
- You have opened up the prison of my life, and now I'm free.
- In you, my darling, I've discovered the joy of loving.
- You have all my love. And with it, all of me.
- I composed the most beautiful love letter during the early-morning hours when I couldn't sleep. It perfectly told you what's in my heart for you—all my love—in words, elegant and true. But now I'm awake, and it is gone. How shall I ever tell you what's in my heart?
- You have become my one true love. I hear music. This could make a wonderful line in a song, right?

PART FIVE

Care and Concern Messages

*A greeting card sent with your handwritten message
expressing your care and concern for someone you know
who is experiencing some kind of trouble—an illness, an
accident, or a loss—can be a light in the darkness. The
fact that you extend a hand of comfort and care will be
particularly meaningful to the recipient. It says, "I see
you're hurting," "I care," and "I'm concerned about you."
It can also say, "I'm here for you, and I want to offer
encouragement, succor, and help."*

Think of your message as a way of cheering and relieving the person who will recover to become whole again. Think of it as a hug to the very distressed person who faces an uncertain future; or one who has suffered a loss.

Get Well

Sending a message to an ill or injured person takes some sensitivity, care, and preparation. It will be much more meaningful if you can make a personal connection, say something positive about the person, and give sincere good wishes for wellness and an anticipated future event.

Message Etiquette

Sensitive, considerate, respectful, and encouraging are the important points in writing your message. Here are some suggestions to help you get there:

1. Focus on the person you're writing to. Tune in to her personality and desires before purchasing your greeting card. If you know someone only casually—like through a parent association committee at your children's school—but *do* know that she's a very private person, use that information to influence the card you purchase and the message you write. You want your card to respect her

privacy and personality, and appropriately reflect the relationship between you—caring, but not overly familiar.
Certainly not invasive.

**2. Know a few facts about the accident or illness before
sending off a card, if possible.** And, if you can easily do so
without being invasive, check on the patient's prognosis.
This, too, will inform your selection of a card and guide
your message.

**3. Make a meaningful personal connection with the
person you are writing to.** If you're in a book club together, you might reference her valuable input, or insightful
contributions. If she's a terrific mom, a wonderful gardener,
a great athlete, or a terrific boss, you may use a brief anecdotal tidbit to underscore your connection and your
appreciation for her skills and person.

4. Offer encouragement. This could be a simple statement
for a "speedy recovery," or a very brief sentence or two about
returning to good health. The ill person, or someone who's
just had major surgery, may suffer from a loss of perspective
and feel she may not be able to return to life as she has
known it. You can remind her. If a weekend-warrior athlete
friend is having a hip replacement, for example, and doesn't
feel she'll be able to return to active sports, you might want
to include a sentence about a professional athlete who had
the procedure and is still a star, or report a fact from a scien-
tific study that indicates a very high success rate for the
procedure and a return to an active lifestyle.

But don't lapse into a tale about your own procedure,

or that of your uncle Bob. And certainly don't relate any medical horror stories. This takes the focus off the person you're writing to, and can leave her feeling marginalized, disrespected, anxious, or worse.

If you have cautionary advice you feel is important to her, and can state it positively, you may want to say something like, "I've had the procedure and would be happy to discuss it with you if you want to give me a call," or, "Here's a link to a new report out on the procedure. I thought you might want to review it."

5. Include a statement of hope for a future anticipated event, or relationship. Just a general get-well card to the woman on your PTA committee, with a message that someone mentioned she is dealing with a health issue, your best wishes, and a sentence saying you hope she'll soon be back at committee meetings, is the right tone for a casual acquaintance. Something like: "I missed your thoughtful input at PTA last night. Someone mentioned you've been in the hospital. I'm sending best wishes for your speedy recovery. I hope to see you back in the seat next to mine at October's PTA meeting." (You won't want to mention the fact that you heard she had surgery for an ulcer.)

6. Offer real help that you're able and willing to carry through on. In the case of the woman on your PTA committee, you might offer, "Emma would love to have Jamie over on Friday to play for a couple of hours. If that will work, please call me. I'll pick her up and deliver her home."

Other sorts of help you may want to volunteer might include delivering meals, if the patient is incapacitated and will need to convalesce. It could be walking the dog, caring for her child, or taking over one of her responsibilities at work. It's important to be specific about what you're offering, and be totally willing and able to complete the task in a manner that frees her from having to be involved, or worry about it.

QUOTABLE QUOTES

I reckon being ill as one of the great pleasures of life,
provided one is not too ill and is not obliged
to work till one is better.
—*Samuel Butler,* English essayist and author

One of the most difficult things to contend
with in a hospital is the assumption on the part
of the staff that because you have lost your
gall bladder you have also lost your mind.
—*Jean Kerr,* American author and playwright

I enjoy convalescence. It is the part
that makes the illness worthwhile.
—*George Bernard Shaw,* Irish-born English playwright

The first thing about being a patient—
you have to learn patience.
—*Oliver Sacks,* English-American physician and author

We are so fond of one another,
because our ailments are the same.
—*Jonathan Swift,* Irish priest and satirist

If Mr. McMurphy doesn't want to take his medication orally, I'm sure we can arrange that he can have . . .

—Nurse Ratched character, *One Flew over the Cuckoo's Nest*

Suggested Messages

GENERAL

- Here's to a very speedy recovery! We need you back at your desk and making those client calls. No one does it better.
- Smiles, they say, are the best medicine. Here's a giant one for you from your grandson. He's going to hold you to that trip to the zoo next month! So, please get all well real soon.
- We simply can't do without you. Get well really soon!
- What? Our Nana is sick? When I mentioned this to [Name], he had this to say: "Noooo," his favorite two-year-old word. And we all agree. That simply won't do. We need, need, need our Nana to come visit us in June. Get all better "weally, weally fast . . ."
- OK? Here's a big kiss, and a superbig family hug from all of us. It contains all our love for you to get well soon.
- We've gotten the bad news at the office. And in addition to everyone sending their heartfelt wishes for your speedy recovery, I'm sending my special wish that you'll be completely well by conference time. I can't imagine anyone but you doing the welcoming role.
- We've got our ear to the grapevine, and we're waiting to hear you're better, better, better, and well. Now let's hear it!
- You're simply too precious to be anything but superrobust.

- Here's a pocketful of sunshine to brighten your day, and to help you get back into full bloom.
- Everyone is feeling a bit <u>ill</u> at the news that you're under the weather. You're far too important here to keeping things running properly. Plus, we just like you around. Get well soon.
- Rest, I'm told, is the very best medicine for a whole lot of whatever ails you. I'm hoping you'll use it in abundance to get yourself recharged, refreshed, reinvigorated, and feeling <u>really, really</u> great again.
- You're far too special a person to be sick. Hope to see you on the well list and in glowing health very soon.
- There's nothing wrong here that a renewed and well [Name] couldn't cure. Hope your recovery is right on track. We all miss you, and wish you the best.
- A spoonful of medicine, a whole lot of rest, and a grueling six weeks of rehab—I'm sure that's just what the doctor ordered for your shoulder. I know you'll be a superstar at all of it, but I'd like to organize rides to school for the kids, and rides to rehab for you, if that's helpful. I've already heard from a dozen people who want to help. I'll call you Thursday to learn what you'd like. But above all, we're all wishing you a full and complete recovery.
- I'm hoping you feel a bit better, and healthier each day.
- You only have to do today. Tomorrow you'll be one day closer to completely well.
- I know you, and I'm sure you'll be back on your feet and dancing the tango in no time. Maybe even wearing that cast. Meanwhile, I'm ready to help in any way you'd like. Any Thursday errands or grocery shopping I can do? I'll call you on Wednesday.

- No one feels totally well when they're sick. So, get well soon.
- We all miss you here. (No one else knows how to update the Website.) Get well, and come back! Real soon!
- Our healthy thoughts, prayers, and wishes for a return of your usual robust self.
- There's a decided gap in our girlfriends' happy circle when you're away. You always add the sunshine. Get well soon.
- OK, I'll admit it. There is a teeny-tiny bit of selfishness in my good wishes for you to be back in the pink of health—I really, really miss you. No one can fill your shoes; especially that pair of old Nikes you keep under the desk for walking at noon. (There haven't even been any offers!)
- You're the smile of good morning, the "have a nice lunch," and the steady hand that keeps this place running smoothly. Yes, you are greatly missed here. Get well. And soon. You know you're indispensable.
- Yes, I readily admit it: things don't run well without you. But more to the point, we all miss you, care about you, and want you to get totally well.
- You're in my thoughts and prayers. I'm counting the days till you're completely well.
- Hospital food is just one of the incentives for getting out of there as soon as possible, I'm sure. Nursing staff visits every 15 minutes through the night is another. But here's hoping that our wishes for a healthy and happy recovery are dozens and dozens more. We all send our best.
- Roses are red, violets are blue, and so are we without you! Gosh, we all miss you, and hope you bounce back

soon. Your side of the tennis ladder is collapsing without you.

- You know what? Everyone who's been in bed a few days feels weak as a kitten. You'll bounce back to your old vim and vigor very fast. How about I come by in the late afternoons Monday, Wednesday, and Friday after work and we walk a few blocks at my snail's pace? You must promise not to speed away from me, OK? I'll call Sunday to learn what will help.

- It's always darkest before . . . the stitches come out? (I know, now it's glue or staples.) I'm sure you're about to turn the corner and experience the happy sunlight of healing. It couldn't happen to a nicer person! Wishing you wellness in abundance.

- We continue to pray for God's loving care and your return to resounding good health.

- His eye is on the sparrow, and we know His gentle loving arms are wrapped around you. We continue to remember you in our prayers.

- Our wish is that this bad patch will soon be over, and you'll be back to the days of clover. We all miss your ready smile and quick humor. (Oh, and the donuts on Monday mornings.)

WHEN THE NEWS ISN'T GOOD

Message Etiquette

Be extra-sensitive. It's important to be aware that those who are suffering a very dire illness, and/or are facing an uncertain future, may be near the brink of being overtaxed. You'll see that the following messages contain suggestions about ways to help, and requests for permission to visit, etc. The casual reader may think these details could better be covered in a telephone call, but it's far more considerate to put them in writing in your greeting card, and then follow up with a telephone call; or wait for a response (if that's what you've proposed). The reason for this approach is twofold: the ill person may have a real need to feel in control of something in her life, and with this approach, you're giving her that power. Second, she is undoubtedly also suffering the effects of being heavily medicated, anxious, exhausted, and often unable to cope with making immediate decisions. If you write these things in your greeting card, you are giving her the best opportunity to decide what she wants you to do, when she wants you to visit, or if and how she wants the help you're offering. This is the soul of real empathy—not to be confused with the doltish approach of *saying* you know how the ill person feels; or the completely insensitive approach of marginalizing the ill person's suffering by launching into your own "related" story about your uncle Bob. Again, be extra-sensitive, tune in to the ill person's needs and desires, and just be there.

QUOTABLE QUOTES

. . . To live is to suffer,
to survive is to find meaning in
the suffering.
—*Viktor Frankl,* Austrian neurologist and psychiatrist

Hope is the thing with feathers
That perches in the soul,

And sings the tune without the words,
And never stops at all.
—*Emily Dickinson*, American poet

Suggested Messages

- It's an ugly word—"cancer." But I've never known you to shrink from a real challenge. We're all betting on your resilience and fight. In case we haven't said it recently: You're very important to us. We care what happens to you. And we all want you around for a very long time to come. We're sending you our best wishes and prayers.

- Do you know what a huge, positive influence you've been on so many lives? Probably not. You've always been the pillar of quiet fortitude from whom so many have drawn strength. I'm sure that's how you're facing this challenge. There are many of us sending our very best wishes. But do lean on us for a change. I'll call [Spouse or Friend's Name] on Thursday to see if we can arrange a series of brief visits or outings. Whatever you'd like to do, and feel up to.

- You are in my heart, on my mind, and in my prayers. I'm keeping in touch with [Spouse or Friend's Name] to learn what you might like for me to do to put legs on my thoughts and prayers. Meanwhile, here are some of our favorite poems.

- I know you won't ever give up. That's the kind of determination that has marked everything you've ever done. But do call on your friends—on me—whenever there's something you need. How about a Saturday ball game?

- The news may not be good, but I know your hope, strength, and resolve have never faltered. I just wanted to say I'm here for you, [Name]. Would it be helpful if I came for a week when you return home? My cooking isn't gourmet, but I listen well, can be very quiet around the house, and would love to take you to some of your favorite haunts. It's been way too long since we've done a theater performance, for example.

- We were disappointed to hear that the current therapy wasn't going as well as we'd all like, but we are optimistic that this new treatment will show better results.

  We want you both to know that if there is anything we can do to help lighten the load, you only need ask.

  [Caregiver Name], if you need to get away for a while, I'll be happy to come and take care of [Patient Name] and do my Nurse Ratched impersonation. That way, [Caregiver], you can get some R & R. Or, [Patient Name], if you, or both of you for that matter, need some time in a different locale, we would be delighted to have you come here for as long as you'd like.

  Please let us know. We love you both and want to do whatever we can to lighten your load.

- I heard the news isn't good. But I know that you're a person who has so often beat the odds. And I'm fully expecting that you'll do it again. With flying colors!

- We believe in miracles! And we're praying for one with your name on it. I'll call you on Thursday to see if I might come over for our weekly chess session. I'll bring the Ben & Jerry's Chunky Monkey.

- My personal list of heroes is very short; and you, my dear friend, are vying for the number-one spot. I've always particularly admired your courage; but never more than now. Will you allow me to drive you to the Grand

Canyon—that trip we've talked about so often? It would be an honor to see it with you.

- You've been a role model to so many, and I'm sure now in this present situation you'll teach everybody you know just how to face this kind of crisis. But do let your friends return a tiny bit of the riches you've added to our lives. We'd like to help you—for a change—by forming a carpool to take you to treatment sessions. I'll call you on Tuesday to see what you need. We'd also like to take you to a series of lunches, whenever you're ready.

- I'm praying that you'll have painless days of clarity and peace. I'd like to come read to you three afternoons a week for an hour, if you'd enjoy that. We could perhaps get through some of that poetry we've been saying we want to read again. Would Tuesday, Thursday, and Saturday at 4:00 P.M. work?

- I'm sorry, [Name], that I haven't told you nearly often enough how important you've been in my life. You've been a rock to me—the person I've always known I can count on. Will you please let me do something for you? I'm thinking particularly about helping you complete that memoir. I can set up the reviewers and do the editing. I could start next week.

Special Messages

ILL OR INJURED CHILD

- Hickory, dickery dock, the mouse ran up the clock,
  And he told me you're not feeling so very well.
  Here's my wish for you, [Name]:
  Very soon, down he'll run

And tell me you're all well again.

And you're out playing with your friends.

- Who likes that awful-tasting medicine?

Not you.

But it may be the very thing that will get you all well again, and ready for our camping trip.

Just so I'm sure to be ready, would you please write me a list of all the things you can think of that we'll need to take? I've enclosed a list to start.

- Everyone at the Cub Scouts meeting was unhappy to hear you're sick. But you'll still have plenty of time to get your project done for the next meeting. I got your supplies for you. Give me a call when you're ready for me to bring them over.

- Once upon a time there was a little girl—well, not that little and getting bigger each day—who fell off her bike and broke her leg. At first, it hurt and hurt. But then the doctor fixed it and put on a colorful cast. And very soon, she'll be out riding her bike again!! Hooray! [Name], I hear you are being very brave. And you're getting better every day. Here are some special stickers for your cast. You must have quite a collection. Email me a picture, will you?

- No one likes being in the hospital very much, it's true. Sure, we're glad we have hospitals to fix things that aren't quite well, but we want to go home as soon as possible. So, the very best advice is to do all the things the doctor says, and you'll be out and playing ball again real soon.

- Here's an IOU for one hot fudge sundae as soon as you're well. Maybe by a week from Friday after school?

- I'm sending you a riddle book to help you while away the time until you're up and skateboarding again.
- I'm thinking there aren't many boys your age who come out of the hospital smiling. But you did! As soon as you're all well, we'll be trying for one of those bass in the lake. OK? Here's a picture of a record-winner that was caught yesterday. Isn't this a beauty?
- Guess what's coming to town? Yes, the circus. And I have two tickets with your name on them—one for you, and one for a friend. That gives you five weeks to get ready for the big top! I'm betting your favorite performer is going to be the dancing bear.

Loss

We can't experience real growth or change in our lives without experiencing loss, but few of us welcome it. Grieving is painful, and the process is often protracted. And although grief has its seasons, the length and intensity of each of these varies greatly with each person who must weather it to arrive—changed—at the other side. It must be said, too, that the expression of grief is unique to each person and each relationship.

The first phase of grief is shock, numbness, denial, and disbelief. These may arrive in succession, or in some cocktail combination that produces a near paralysis.

Then there are phases of experiencing the pain of the loss, as the reality sets in. Here, the bereaved must process the loss, and somehow, work through it.

Hopefully, in the final phase of loss, the bereaved arrives at a state of resolution, acceptance, and healing. But the journey often takes detours, regressions, and hits back roads between phases, as well.

And it's important to say that grief isn't linear: sometimes long after the bereaved feels she has accepted the loss and is starting to heal, she will be hit with another wave of pain so acute that she feels like the process is starting all over again. This often occurs on those days that were significant to the bereaved and the deceased, like a wedding anniversary or a birthday, or being in a special place where they spent time together.

When you learn of someone else's loss, you will immediately want to connect to the grieving person, and offer comfort. But you may also be afraid of saying, doing, or writing the wrong thing; you don't want your words to further injure. So, not knowing what will be helpful, you may feel you're in a kind of silent, limbo state.

Greeting cards are, for this reason, very helpful. And so are the following guidelines from hundreds of grieving people who've told me what they found most comforting during their process of grieving.

Message Etiquette

Review the phases of grief, then follow these steps to help you write words that lend comfort. You may not address all of these in your message, or use them exactly in this order, but consider them in adjusting your message to the stage and needs of the grieving person.

You may want to write a complete letter of sympathy, or add a personal message to a greeting card that is printed with words you want to convey. However, do write at least a few lines from your own heart to make a very personal and meaningful connection with the person who is grieving.

Sending a condolence message by email is fraught with difficulties. It may be perceived by the grieving person as lacking the proper respect or weight for such a loss. And it does. But if there is an immediate message you need to convey, and you are certain that the grieving person will be using her email, you may want to send a brief email or texted message, and follow it with a mailed sympathy message.

Send your message of condolence by email *only* if it's the best way to convey your message to the person when: (1) you know this person primarily in cyberspace; or, (2) you need to get an immediate message to her. Always send a formal handwritten condolence message by mail, too.

If in doubt, try to determine the need to email your message by carefully considering these questions:

1. Will your email message be welcomed by the grieving person? Would *she* send *you* a message of condolence by email; and/or is there something you need to convey immediately—before you can reach her by telephone or speak to her in person? If you need, for example, to convey that you will take care of some immediate arrangement for her, then you may properly email or text that message, in addition to leaving a voice message.

2. Will you be seeing or talking to the person within the next day? If you will, there is undoubtedly no need to send an email or text message.

Here, then, are the steps to sending your handwritten message of sympathy:

1. **Acknowledge the loss.** Set the tone of your message by stating that you have learned of the loss, and name it. But first, if possible, check the facts. It's appropriate to state your own emotion, but don't lapse into overcharged terms like "the worst news ever," "devastated," "completely overcome with grief," and so on.

2. **Make a statement of sympathy.** This should be aimed at telling the grieving person that you care. If this is a death, and you knew the deceased well, you might frame your statement in terms of the loss both the bereaved and you are experiencing. But it's never appropriate to turn the focus on yourself and a loss you've experienced, in an attempt to show empathy by comparing the loss with one of your own. Instead of your intended goal, this could sideline your message or make the bereaved feel her loss is being marginalized.

3. **Make a positive statement.** For a deceased person, you may want to state some of her character strengths you admire, or the faith that guided her life. Use something that says the deceased was a valued person.

4. **Share a positive memory that illustrates your statement.** Make it as specific as possible. Serious or humorous, a very brief "story" will be appreciated by the bereaved.

5. **Focus on the bereaved.** Remind the bereaved of her own personal character strengths that will allow her to survive this very dark time. Remember that loss can make the

strongest person feel vulnerable, unable to cope, and often helpless. It is often beneficial to use a statement the deceased used to describe the bereaved.

6. Offer your help and support. But be sure to offer only what you are able and willing to carry through on without a lot of direction or input from the bereaved. She will undoubtedly be unable to make many decisions. Make it as concrete as possible. State your offer in very clear terms, with any limitations you need to impose. Then follow up. Opaque and general offers aren't comforting, and smack of insincerity.

QUOTABLE QUOTES

We give him back to you, O God, who gave him to us.
Yet, as you did not lose him in giving,
so we do not lose him by his return.
—*Anonymous*

Life is eternal; and love is immortal;
and death is only a horizon;
and a horizon is nothing save the limit of our sight.
—*Rossiter W. Raymond,* American poet, author,
hymn writer, miner, and engineer

They that love beyond the world cannot be separated by it.
Death cannot kill what never dies.
—*William Penn,* English-American colonist and philanthropist

Death leaves a heartache no one can heal;
Love leaves a memory no one can steal.
—*From a headstone in Ireland*

In the middle of difficulty lies opportunity.
—*Albert Einstein,* German-born American physicist

To live in hearts we leave behind is not to die.
—*Thomas Campbell,* Scottish poet

Like the voice of a bird singing in the rain, let grateful
memories survive in the hour of darkness.
—*Robert Louis Stevenson,* Scottish poet and author

Most of the important things in the world have been
accomplished by people who have kept on trying
when there seemed to be no hope at all.
—*Dale Carnegie,* American industrialist and philanthropist

Though nothing can bring back the hour
Of splendor in the grass, of glory in the flower;
We will grieve not, rather find
Strength in what remains behind.
—*William Wordsworth,* English poet

I know for certain that we never lose the people we love,
even to death. They continue to participate in every act,
thought, and decision we make.
—*Leo Buscaglia,* American author

I would rather have such a memorial of one I dearly love,
than the noblest Artist's work ever produced.
—*Elizabeth Barrett Browning,* English poet

Even in our sleep, pain which cannot forget
falls drop by drop upon the heart, and in our own
despair, against our will, comes wisdom
through the awful grace of God.
—*Aeschylus,* Greek playwright

Death is not extinguishing the light,
It is only putting out the lamp because dawn has come.
—*Rabindranath Tagore,* Indian religious leader, poet, and philosopher

God is our refuge and our strength,
a very present help in trouble.
—*Bible. Psalms 46:1*

Death is nothing at all.
It does not count.
I have only slipped away into the next room.
Everything remains as it was.
The old life that we lived so fondly
together is untouched, unchanged.
Whatever we were to each other, that we are still.
Call me by the old familiar name.
Speak of me in the easy way, which you always used.
Put no sorrow in your tone.
Laugh as we always laughed at the little jokes
that we enjoyed together.
Play, smile, think of me, pray for me.

Let my name be ever the household word
that it always was.
Let it be spoken without effort
Life means all that it ever meant.
It is the same as it ever was.
There is unbroken continuity.
Why should I be out of mind because I am out of sight?
I am but waiting for you, for an interval,
somewhere very near, just around the corner.
All is well. Nothing is hurt; nothing is lost.
One brief moment and all will be as it was before.
How we shall laugh at the trouble of parting,
when we meet again.
—*Henry Scott Holland,* English
philosopher and reformer

Some of our best living is done
through those we leave behind.
—*Anonymous*

Suggested Messages
SYMPATHY—THE LOSS OF AN ADULT LOVED ONE

- Our sincerest condolences at the loss of your dear [Name].
- With loving thoughts for you at the loss of your dear [Name].
- Please know that we are remembering you and honoring the memory of [Name].
- Loved so much; gone too soon. We are holding you close in our thoughts and prayers.
- [Name] will remain in our hearts forever.
- Sent with our love and remembrance.

- We pray that God enfolds you with His love during this time of grieving.
- With love and abiding hugs.
- Words are certainly inadequate to express the sadness we feel by the passing of [Name]. We are here for you in this time of sorrow. With our sincerest sympathy.
- May peace and comfort be yours during this dark time.
- [Hand-Delivered to the Home and Given to a Close Relative]

[Name], I heard today at church the very sad news that [Name] lost his life in a motorcycle accident. I telephoned, but got no answer.

My heart is filled with sympathy for you and for the boys. I didn't know [Name] well, but was always very impressed that your boys loved him deeply, and were filled with admiration and respect for their dad. That's the true test of a man's worth—to be so loved by his children. And that impression of their respect was reinforced last June at a Sunday-school softball game when [Name] mediated a heated debate about a call of "out" at first by telling the young ump, "We should do what's fair. The runner was definitely there before the ball."

I can't imagine your pain at this very dark time. But I do know you are a woman of unshakeable faith and inner strength. And I'm sure you will also draw strength from your love for [Name].

I'd like to organize meals for you and the boys for a month. Each member of the family club will bring in dinner each evening at 6:00 P.M. I'd also like to offer hospitality to family members arriving in town for the funeral; and a light luncheon for those attending the funeral, afterward in the fellowship hall. I'll call tomorrow to check with you, or your mother, about this.

Please know that we are keeping you in our prayers, and stand ready to help in any way you may need. We love you and the boys, we are your church family, please let us help carry your heavy burden.

- I was so sorry to learn at the office this morning that your mother has passed away, [Name], and you've had to return to Michigan to make funeral arrangements. It's always too soon to lose your mother; my heartfelt sympathy to you.

  I didn't know your mom, of course, but knowing you, I'm sure she was a wonderful person of high principles— because she raised such a wonderful daughter.

  May the love you shared, and your memories of her, sustain you during this time of grieving.

  Please think of me as your work support person, and call me if I can take over any client contact meetings while you're away.

  You are in my prayers.

- [Name], I was saddened to hear about the passing of your mom. When I was growing up, she was my idea of the perfect Mother. And the very best cook ever. How I enjoyed coming to your house on those Sunday afternoons, and smelling her stewed chicken and buttermilk biscuits. Then she'd always invite me to stay for dinner—an invitation I secretly hoped would come each time. And whenever there was a parent participation activity at school, I knew I'd see her front and center. And I looked forward to her ready greeting and smile.

She left some very important—and impossible—shoes to fill. I can't imagine how much you'll miss her. I'm putting together some of the memories of her from our classmates that I'm hoping will be meaningful to you. I'll send it over on Friday.

- Our thoughts and prayers are with you in this very difficult time.
- We were so saddened to hear of the loss of the love of your life. He was a prince of a man, everyone who knew him knew that, and we share just a fraction of the void and sorrow you must be feeling. Our thoughts and prayers are with you.
- We are thinking of you, and holding you close with warmth, sympathy, and thoughts of comfort during this dark time of loss.
- We have all lost a wonderful friend. But you have lost a soul mate. Our hearts are heavy with our grief, and with sorrow for you. And we will be thinking of you with thoughts of sympathy.
- We love you, and will miss [Name] so very much. You are in our thoughts and prayers as you try to process your grief. Please know you can call us at any time of the day or night—even if you just want someone to come and sit with you.
- We've all lost a valued colleague. But I know you've also lost a business partner and a very close friend. I'm so sorry for the pain this is causing you in so many ways. You're in my thoughts, and I'm hoping your memories of [Name] are a comfort to you. He always spoke so admiringly of you.

- "No one ever told me that grief felt so like fear," C. S. Lewis wrote in *A Grief Observed*. I'm holding you close in my thoughts and prayers as you grapple with your loss. I don't know what else to offer as help, but I'm a great listener if you want to talk. Call my cell phone day or night.

- I heard the very sad news this morning that our dear [Name] is gone from us. But not really gone, a tiny epiphany informed me. Although we all grieve with you, at the same time we are so aware that all around the world there are lives that are enriched and enlightened from having known him. He helped so many. I sensed the shining of thousands of lights that [Name] ignited.

  We will all miss him so. Please let us hold you close during this terrible time; and call us when you'd like to talk about [Name], or need something.

- C. S. Lewis wrote after the death of his wife, "Her absence is like the sky, spread over everything." I know you must feel the same about losing [Name]. I know I can't lessen your pain; but please know that there are many who care. I'm keeping you close in my prayers.

- [Name], you were a wonderful wife to [Name]. He said it often, as well as, "She's my rock." But you don't have to be strong all by yourself. Your friends are here; please let us help.

- I was so saddened to hear that you lost your precious husband. And we lost a dear friend. Our loss can't be compared to yours; but we all will surely miss him very much. I loved the way he often said of you, "She's the best human being I know."

You're in my heart, [Name]. My prayer is that your memories of [Name] will be some comfort during such a difficult time.

- I've never known a more generous person than [Name]. Her heart for volunteering and caring for others seemed to be bottomless. I so often marveled at her efforts, like the day I volunteered with her at the children's nursery. I told her she looked a bit tired, and she finally admitted that the nursery was her third volunteer effort for that day! So many will miss her loving heart and generous spirit, but none more than you, I'm sure. I'm keeping you in my daily prayers during this time of grieving.

- It doesn't seem possible that [Name] is gone. She was the most alive person I've ever known. But as she so often said, "I'm making sure I'll live forever by giving of myself to others." I know she gave immensely to me. Now, I'll try to share that giving with others.

    My thoughts are with you during this painful period of loss.

SYMPATHY—LOSS OF A CHILD

- [Name] and I were so saddened to hear of [Name]'s fatal accident. Our hearts ache for you; we can't imagine your pain at losing your beloved baby. Such a joy and beautiful tiny person [Name] was.

    No two parents ever loved a child more. If there is perfect love, you personified it. And I saw the love she returned to you. Our prayers are with you in this very dark hour.

- There simply aren't any words that can restore the loss of hope a parent experiences when a baby dies. We grieve with you at the passing of little [Name]. It's so out of the natural order of life.

We hold you in our thoughts and prayers that you may be wrapped in your love for each other, and the love you bestowed on [Name] to see you through this time of grieving.

- Nothing in life can prepare a parent for what you've suffered in losing your precious baby, [Name]. I'm so very sorry. Words are so inadequate for such suffering.

  I wish I were wise enough to impart some comfort; and you weren't too wounded to hear it. But I can only assure you that you were wonderful parents, and [Name] was a perfect angel. I have a very special place for you in my heart, and you both are in my prayers.

- There was never a son who better reflected the wonderful job of parenting he'd had than your son, [Name]. I know how very proud of him you are, and how much he loved you. He was a wonderful young man who'd taken his place in the world, and gave so much to so many.

  We are so sorry he was called away from this world, and you, at such a young age. And we're so sad that you're left with such sorrow.

  When you are ready, we'd like to talk with you about all the things your wonderful son accomplished. Until then, our thoughts and prayers are with you.

- We were so sorry to learn that [Name] lost his life in Iraq. We all know, of course, that our children weren't given to us to possess; but are gifts from God, only loaned to us and entrusted to our care for a season. And we'd like to go on record as saying you two did your jobs so very well. You produced a wonderful son, [Name], who loved his fellow man and his country. And gave his all. He will certainly live on in the hearts of many.

- Joan Didion wrote in *The Year of Magical Thinking*, "Grief turns out to be a place none of us know until we reach it." We don't know the depth of your suffering, but we are keeping you in our thoughts and prayers at this very difficult time.

- We were so sorry to hear of the passing of [Name]. She was a beautiful person, and so very brave. I remember before her last hospitalization she said, "I think of each operation as one more step toward my goal of getting whole."

    You two were the most giving of parents, who nurtured your daughter in every possible way. Our prayer is only that the measure of your love for each other and for [Name]—and hers for you—may embrace and hold you in this dark time of loss.

- With deepest sympathy, I send my love. It's simply not fair that [Name] was taken from you so soon. She was the most delightful child; always with a ready smile, and ever curious about everything.

    And your love for her was wonderful to witness. As was hers for you.

    My hope is that your wonderful memories of this very special child are some consolation in your grief. You are in my prayers.

Message Etiquette
AFTER-LOSS THANK-YOU NOTES

You will want to express your thanks to those who extended condolences and messages of sympathy, and performed acts of kindness to you and your family during your initial grieving process. That will include those who sent messages or funeral flowers; attended the visitation, funeral, or memorial service; made a donation in honor of the deceased; or brought meals or did other things on your behalf during this time.

To ease what may feel a huge burden during a very difficult time, this is a job that may be done by the entire family together, and one inclusive message of thanks sent. To this message, you'll want to add a sentence or two about the specific gift or act that the recipient offered.

The general etiquette rule is that the thank-you message be sent within two to three months after the funeral or memorial service. But if all the family members have gathered for the funeral or memorial service, you may want to have them each sign the thank-you notes while they are together. Or, one family member may sign on behalf of the entire family.

If you do this at the time of the funeral, or do it later, your family may find this a good time and way to support each other, share some of their memories of the deceased, and grieve together.

If you prepared a memorial statement for the deceased that was distributed at the service, and you're writing to someone who was unable to attend, you may want to include a copy with your thank-you message. Or, you may want to have a special thank-you message or a bereavement verse printed in thank-you notes, then add individual thank-you messages, and send these.

Suggested Messages

- [Name], thank you for attending [Name]'s memorial service. It was a great comfort having you there to pay tribute to his life.

- [Name], we couldn't have said a proper good-bye to [Name] without you. Thank you for being there, for serving as an usher, and for your very kind and funny words of remembrance you shared at the memorial service.

- [Name], Dad thought the world of you. He so often said, "After God made [Name], He threw away the mold. She's perfect." I know you'll miss him, as we do. And I'm sure he's smiling now and waiting for us.

- We don't have the proper words to express our thanks for your kindnesses during the days after [Name] passed on. We were in such a bewildering and dark place; we couldn't have made it through without you. You were both comfort and quiet orchestration in getting the memorial service organized, the meals brought in, and hospitality arranged. Our whole family is greatly indebted to you. Thank you for such grace and compassion.

- Thank you for attending [Name]'s memorial service, and for taking care of the [name the task] details. Please know that your kindness during this very difficult time has meant a great deal to our entire family.

- Thank you for all your kindness during [Name]'s memorial service. Loving [Name] was so easy, such a delight she was. Missing her is very difficult. And thoughts of her are everywhere and bittersweet—a pleasure and a pain to recall. I know you'll miss her, as we will.

- The last time I heard [Name] speak, it was of you, and your trip with her to Spain. Thank you for sharing in remembering her, and for the thoughts and memories you shared with all of us.
- Thank you for joining with us in our tribute to [Name]. We all miss him immensely, but we know he's still with us: our memories of him will last. We were so fortunate to have had him in our lives.
- Thank you for your card and the kind words. I know you are grieving his loss, too, and you are in our thoughts.
- The generosity and caring of friends like you during this time of the loss of [Name] have been a great help. We loved him so, and are gratified to know so many others did as well.

  The whole family would like to thank you for the (card, flowers, gift, meals, etc.) you sent; and for your loving support.
- There are simply no words to express our thanks for the sympathy you have extended in the (card, flowers, acts of kindness). Our whole family is deeply grateful. It was exactly what [Name] would have chosen.
- You have been a rock and a source of comfort during these dark days of mourning. Thank you for each and every kindness you rendered. We know you are grieving, too, and we are thinking about you.

Message Etiquette
END OF AN ENGAGEMENT—ANNOUNCEMENT

Although there is seldom a formal announcement of the end of an engagement, you will undoubtedly be writing to inform friends and relatives about it as a social courtesy. It's best to make a simple statement of the fact, and treat any other details on a need-to-know basis. You may not want to belabor the fact or go into the details. It's your choice.

Suggested Messages

- I just wanted to tell you that [Name] and I have broken our engagement.
- [Name] and I won't be getting married on July 21 as planned. We have broken our engagement.
- I'm sorry to tell you that [Name] and I have decided to cancel our engagement.

Message Etiquette

END OF AN ENGAGEMENT—RESPONSIVE MESSAGE

It's best to identify with the person informing you of the broken engagement. Don't pry, or ask questions. You may, however, want to offer comfort or just listen, with something like, "If you need a confidential ear to vent into, please call me anytime." Or, "If you'd like to get away for a weekend, please consider coming for a visit."

As with any loss, you may want to send a personal note or a greeting card with a short message of regret and encouragement.

Suggested Messages

- [Name], I was sorry to hear that you and [Name] won't be getting married as planned. I'm sure this has been a time of real distress and upheaval for you coming to this decision.

  I've known you to come through many difficult situations much stronger than when you went into them; and I'm sure this is one from which you'll emerge whole and happy. I'm sure it doesn't feel that way right now. Please be kind to yourself, and give yourself some time to process this loss, and then to heal.

You know I'm available to talk, should you want to have a listening ear.

- This sucks. I'm sorry that you must experience this very sad time. But I know you'll emerge like the phoenix. I've seen you do it at other times, and in other circumstances—obviously, not these.

   What I found helpful during my divorce was realizing that the sun <u>will</u> come up tomorrow. I know there's love and light in your future. You'll choose to look for it, and walk toward it to the place of happiness you so richly deserve. But do give yourself the gift of time. And do know that I'm holding you in my thoughts and prayers.

- It made my heart ache to read your news. I'm so sorry you're hurting. I know you've put your heart and soul into this relationship.

   I'm sure you will again show the kind of courage you have in the past to open yourself to what comes next. And I'm equally certain that there are wonderful things ahead for you.

Message Etiquette
DIVORCE—ANNOUNCEMENT

In telling friends of your divorce, it's best to make a simple statement, and if you don't wish to discuss the details, make that clear, too. You are not obliged to give any more information than you wish to, and you'll never regret saying too much if you don't.

Suggested Messages

- I just wanted to let you know that [Name] and I are, unfortunately, divorcing. I will be moving to 155 E. Appleton, #45, Madison, Wisconsin, 00000, next week. My cell phone number will remain the same. [Name] will be remaining at this address.

  Maybe it seems cowardly to tell you in a personal note, but I can't at this moment face saying it out loud. And, no, I don't want to talk about it at this time. Perhaps later.

- I wanted you to hear this directly from me, before you hear it from someone else: [Name] and I are getting a divorce. It will be effective May 1.

  I don't want to share any details at this time, and I'll let you know by telephone as soon as I know where I'll be locating.

- I thought I should tell you that [Name] and I are starting divorce proceedings. I'll be remaining at this address, but more than that I can't—and don't wish to—discuss right now. I know you'll defer to my wishes on this, and keep this confidential for the time being.

  I know you and [Name] were friends before we met, but I hope we can also remain friends.

  Thank you in advance for your understanding.

Message Etiquette

RESPONDING TO A DIVORCING PERSON

Use the same guidelines as for the broken engagement. It's best to express no opinions, but to just state your support for the person. It's also wise to refrain from making derogatory comments about the other divorcing partner. If couples reunite, a friend who made such comments will definitely be out of the relationship.

Suggested Messages

- I was saddened to hear your news. I know how difficult this time can be, and I feel terrible for you.

  Of course we'll always be friends. I'll wait to hear from you after your move, but please know I'm here for you and available to talk—completely confidentially, if you wish—anytime.

- It's never easy to go through a divorce; and it's much more difficult when there are children involved. I'm so sorry you [Spouse Name] and the children are suffering this.

  I'd be happy to have [Name] and [Name] over in the afternoons after school until 7:00 P.M. for the next four weeks, if that would give you some extra time to look for housing.

  [Name], you are a wonderful and capable person, and I'm sure you've given this every possible chance to work. My best wishes to all of you for a very bright future.

- I'm so sorry to hear that you and [Name] are divorcing. I'm sure it's a decision you both made after very careful consideration, and exhausting every avenue of reconciliation.

  I know how difficult my divorce was, and I empathize with you now during this time of stress and loss.

  You are a wonderful and capable woman, and I want to remind you that there are many, many people who care for you, and wish you every happiness.

I don't know what would be helpful to you right now, but please let me know what you need, and I'll try to help.

- I'm sure this is one of the most difficult decisions you've ever made. And I'm also certain that you made it only after very careful thought and consideration. Still, I'm sure it's a severe shock and a great loss.

    I'll await your call to learn what kind of help you may need. Meanwhile, I'm keeping you in my thoughts and prayers.

- Writing your note had to be very difficult. I admire your resolve and courage. Please don't blame yourself.

    You deserve every happiness, and I feel sure you and [Name] will have happiness in abundance in the not-too-distant future.

Message Etiquette

JOB AND FINANCIAL LOSS ANNOUNCEMENT

When your employment is terminated, or you experience a financial crisis, it's an acute experience of loss. It disrupts life's structure and routine, and often produces disorientation; sometimes it even results in the feeling of losing your identity and feelings of self-worth.

When the condition lingers, it compounds anxiety and stress, and sets up the dynamics for a number of other losses—colleagues, financial security, home, etc. So tied to our careers and financial security are our personal identities that it's not unheard of that the unemployed, or the person who has lost big in the stock market, even feels a sense of shame and failure.

It's usually not a fact you'll want to share in a personal message or note, but when it's important to convey this information to a number of people, you may want to use a personal note to simply state the facts on a need-to-know basis. It can also be helpful to your networking efforts to have friends, relatives, and colleagues know that you'll be looking for new employment.

QUOTABLE QUOTES

Success is how high you bounce when you hit bottom.
—*George Patton*, American military general

These are the times that try men's souls.
—*Thomas Paine*, English-American writer

Suggested Messages

- [Name], sadly, both [Name] and I have been downsized and are mustering our forces to mount a campaign for new positions. Just wanted to let you know that this fact will change our summer plans. Sadly, we'll be unable to visit in August.
- [Name], I wanted to let you know that I have lost my position with [Company Name], and won't be able to go in on the purchase of the cruiser as we had planned.
- I am canceling my membership to the yacht club effective May 1, 0000, due to a financial reversal.

Message Etiquette

JOB OR FINANCIAL LOSS—RESPONSIVE MESSAGE

In sending your personal message to a friend or relative who has suffered this kind of loss, you'll want to reassure the person you're writing to and include words of encouragement. Remember, she may be experiencing anger, anxiety, loss of feelings of self-worth, helplessness, fear, and isolation.

You may also want to offer help; and if you do, be sure it's something you are able and willing to do. Describe what you are offering in explicit and specific terms. Then carry through.

Suggested Messages

- [Name], I'm so sorry about the loss of jobs for you and [Name]. It's a cruel double whammy. We'll certainly miss your visit in August. But we'll look forward to the next time we'll be able to get together. It's always such a delight to have you visit. You know you have a standing invitation.

    You two are among the best in your fields, I've seen both of you in action. I'm sure your talents won't be on the market long.

    Our thoughts and wishes for a very short period of unemployment, and just the right fit in new positions. I do have a couple of contacts I'd like to share with you, and will call you next week to discuss them.

    We're also enclosing a gift card for Whole Foods. This isn't charity, we just want to let you know we care. And we want to pay it backward and forward. Someone gave us one when finances were flagging, and it was nice to know that if we really needed a special treat there was a means for getting it.

You're in our thoughts and prayers here. Let's keep in touch.

- [Name], first let me say that I was so sorry to hear of your job loss. As Dad used to say, "Life is all about taking a punch," and I know you are one of the most resourceful and resilient people I've ever known. This, I'm sure, won't keep you down.

  About that cruiser: not to worry. It's a very postponable dream, and maybe in the future we'll decide again to do it. I'll look forward to that possibility.

  Meanwhile, please know that you can call on me for help during this rough patch. And you know we can still go fishing in the old tub.

- [Name], I and the guys who received your message are all sorry to hear about this financial bump in the road. And we all felt this is no time for you to give up your yacht club membership. Besides, we've been the real beneficiaries of that membership. You've hosted us a zillion times.

  So, we'd like to return your sailing hospitality with a gift of one year's membership. The check is enclosed.

  Best wishes for very smooth financial sailing! We all know you'll be back on an even keel very soon.

Message Etiquette

DEATH OF A PET

Pet people are among some of the kindest and most caring of human beings. And because that is true, they may relate to their pets as others do to a close friend or child. It's different, yes, but, it's often a very close relationship.

The loss of a pet will certainly cause grief. And you can help by offering sympathy and support. Understanding the person's relationship to the pet, and the circumstances of the loss, will allow you to craft your message.

Acknowledge the loss. If possible, say something positive about the pet, and offer words of encouragement for the person. Resist the impulse to suggest that obtaining another pet will diminish or eliminate the loss.

Suggested Messages

- [Name], I was sorry to hear that you have lost your beloved Moppy. He was a prince among cats, and regally reigned over the entire neighborhood from his perch atop your camelback sofa. The whole neighborhood will miss seeing him in your window. And Rags will, for some time, still look for him there when we walk by, and he'll bark a tribute.

  It's never easy to lose a pet. But as you mourn your loss, please remember that there was never a better "cat lady" who created a more loving home than you did for Moppy. He was one very lucky cat to have found you.

  I'm enclosing my favorite picture of Moppy and Rags together in one of their many games of animal chess. I think Moppy is saying, "It's your move, Raggy. But you'd better be careful, I have a secret weapon!"

- Who won't miss the toothy smile, clicking nails, and waving backside of Pouch upon approaching your front door? I was so sorry to hear she's gone.

She was the cleverest of dogs. And a true gourmet! I'll never forget watching her paw that pound of plated butter from the back of the counter, and ever so delicately take a few licks, run her tongue around her face, then give a satisfied grin when she noticed I was watching her.

I know you'll miss her terribly, especially for those cross-country trips. But I'm hoping your memories of her offer some comfort. There was never a dog that had a more wonderful life than you provided for Pouch.

You're in my thoughts, [Name].

• I know your decision to end Purple's suffering was made from a heart full of love for your beloved dog. I would have done—and did—the same thing.

She was a magnificent dog of rare intelligence. I was always sure she'd read the newspaper before bringing it to you each morning. And that look of complete empathy she always wore when you had a migraine—amazing. I can only imagine how sad you are, and how you'll miss her.

I'm keeping you in my thoughts, and hoping that the memories you have of the two of you will help with your grieving.

I'm suggesting that we find a new route for our walks, and that you and I do it together each morning at 6:00 A.M. True, I won't be nearly as much fun to walk with as Purple, but I'll bring in the newspaper when we return, if you like.

• Barney Q. Buckets was a very large dog trapped in a tiny Scottish terrier body. He was never confused by the reflection in the mirror that belied his size. I'll never forget the day he had that Great Dane cowering! In fact, I've found this picture I took, and thought you would enjoy having it. Would that we all had learned that lesson in confidence Barney inherently owned. He taught us a lot of other things, too, didn't he?

I know you feel a vacuum where Barney was, and mourn his loss. It's a very real and big one. My thoughts are with you.

- I'm sorry you have lost Mitzy. I know you must be very sad. I'm thinking healing thoughts for you.
- On the scale of happy pets and their companion people, I know you and Bark had a nearly perfect score. I'm so sorry you've lost him. I know you'll miss him terribly.

    I'm sending my love; you're in my thoughts.
- I can't believe Doodles is gone. I know you're heartbroken.

    I know you haven't given up hope that he'll be found. [Name], you've extended every effort possible to find him. You are truly a wonderful person, as Doodles's loving gaze at you so often testified.

    I'm hoping with you for his return, and thinking loving thoughts. If I can help you put up posters, or make calls to animal shelters, it would make me feel like I'm doing something useful. I'll call in the morning to see if I can make a second or third round of calls, and check the poster sites.
- Few people have experienced the loving companionship you had with Ralph. I know you're grieving.

    I'm hoping that your memories of those happy dog days will be of some comfort.

Message Etiquette

NATURAL DISASTERS, CRIME, AND REALLY DARK TIMES

The person who experiences the trauma of a loss that dramatically impacts their security, identity, and personal safety may suffer the after-effects for a very long period of time. Their first reaction may be fear, shock, violation, rage, and isolation. Other emotional stages of grieving are sure to follow.

Be prepared to stay the course over a long period of time for someone who will need your help. Whatever you write and do, you'll want to be a resource all the way to a complete recovery, so you don't leave the person feeling deserted, which can further injure her.

Your words of comfort are best delivered with the strong muscle of solid help. In fact, few words and much practical help is the best balance.

When someone you know is experiencing trauma and loss, she may not be able to absorb what you say in a telephone call. You may want to follow up with an emailed message and/or a handwritten message to be sure your message has been communicated.

Suggested Messages

- I'm so sorry you had to experience the violation of having your home burglarized and your car stolen. I'm enclosing the keys to the Audi for your use for the next three weeks. It's parked in front of your house.

  If you don't feel safe at home by yourself, please come stay in our guest room for two weeks.

We've found Security Locks at 000-0000, and the HomeSafe security system both excellent. These two things let me sleep at night when Jack is gone on a trip.

I know you're a strong and resilient person and will survive this, but do let me help. And please call me if there's anything else you need. [Hand-delivered after your telephone call.]

- [Name], you've suffered a terrible violation, and I'm so sorry this vile person attacked you. I can't imagine the horror of your experience, or the humiliation of the aftermath of police questioning and medical probing.

  I don't know what, exactly, would be of help to you, but I'm wondering if you would consider coming to stay with us for a month. This might give you time to start your recovery and decide what you want to do.

  I know you're made of good strong stuff, but please do allow us to help. We'll give you as much space as you need, but one or more of us is always around, and ready to listen.

  I'll call you tomorrow and see when you're going to be released from the hospital, and if this will work for you.

- No, I won't say something inane, like you must be a special chosen one to have been picked to suffer something so horrible. I don't believe that. And I'm sure that being able to process this terrible event, grieve, and heal will take a very long time before any of us is able to see any possible positive outcome.

  But I also know you. And I know that you are the strongest and most resourceful person I've ever known. And I know you'll fight to get your life back, and breathe free and without fear again. <u>Yes, I know you will.</u> But do be gentle with yourself, and give yourself time.

- Life isn't fair; I'm so sorry you've had to experience this. And I want to emphasize: it isn't a show of weakness to let others help, it's a sign of strength.

  The reality is that the whole—your network of friends—is stronger than the sum of its parts. I've outlined our plan to help on the sheet I've enclosed. We'll be in for thirty minutes on Thursday to get your approval. And to hear what else you might want us to do to help.

  We all love you, and want to be part of your recovery, if you'll have us.

- Who rescued [Name] from her suicide attempt? Who took [Name] to six weeks of rehab three times a week? Who delivered meals to AIDS patients for three years four nights a week?

  It was the same person who has been there, and "gets it," for dozens and dozens of friends and strangers. Her name is [Name], and now it's her turn to let others—in this case, [Names]—do something for her.

  Please let us help you back to your place in the sun. We'll be there tomorrow with our ideas, for your approval.

- I'm asking God to show you His Face in all of this. It certainly makes no sense to us. But what I do understand and know for a certainty is that happiness will return to you. You are a good and wonderful person, and you'll overcome this very dark day.

- I'm so sorry you're hurting, but I know that happiness will come back to you.

- Don't desert your dreams. Everything you ever wanted and planned for is still possible.

PART SIX

Creating a New Relationship Messages

The people who come into your life become part of your life story—forever. And you become part of theirs. You're written into each other's scripts, and into each other's hearts. Nothing can remove them. They are a part of your history; they leave permanent tracks.

Some psychologists have characterized the relationships of the post "me" (boomer) generations—the X, Y, and Z generations—as being self-centric: "I'm in this relationship for as long as it's good for me." But this view creates only an anemic monologue of a life, and misses the joyous texture and richness of experiencing a full-blown, onstage production of your own life—with all its potential mysterious and fascinating subplots.

Don't shortchange yourself, or those around you, by failing to embrace and build meaningful relationships with those in your life script.

Family Members

Although history is rife with examples of families in conflict, it's also rich with examples of loving families. It's this very inner circle of people in your life you turn to first when good things and bad things happen. They know you, know your history, and know where you came from. And they accept you for all that you've ever been or will be. You have a real stake in each other's lives.

Sure, a few people will *claim* that they have friends who are closer than their relatives, but it's seldom true. It's usually an untested statement, or a defensive one.

However dysfunctional or in disarray they may be, embracing your family members will enrich your life, and theirs. And as to those "package" relatives you get through marriage, they may at first seem just as quirky as some of those with whom you share bloodlines, but the same is true about relating to them.

Message Etiquette

CREATING AN IN-LAW RELATIONSHIP

Enlarging the tent to embrace new family members gained through marriage is a wonderful way to enrich your family, spread the joy, and increase the love. Each person you inherit through marriage shares a very special bond with your spouse, too. What could be a better basis for a great relationship? And each new relative offers the opportunity to have a very special relationship yourself.

In a world with too many things to do, too many places to be, and too many interests competing for your time, it's a real temptation to build barriers instead of bonds with new in-laws. New husbands and new wives, too, often establish a non-relate clause with their mother-in-law, for example, leaving any relationship to her the sole real estate and responsibility of her child. Much happiness is missed in this arrangement. And maybe the mother-in-law is a wonderful person! It's possible. Certainly, any child the couple has in the future will suffer a loss when there isn't a strong in-law bond.

Reject adversarial thoughts and impulses. Embrace the concept of creating strong bonds. Generations ago there was a sense of responsibility on the part of the new son- or daughter-in-law to accept and create a strong and caring personal relationship with the new mother-in-law, and father-in-law. This would be a great tradition to resurrect. Everyone is happier in such a strong multigenerational family. You might want to start the process by writing caring personal messages.

Make an overture of welcome early, and be sure it is sincere.

A personal "welcome to the family" message, if you are a new mother-in-law or family member, is a great place to start—even if you have known the person for a period of time. You may relate something positive about her spouse, extend an invitation of friendship, and close on a positive note that includes your wish for a future relationship. Start with a statement of inclusion and delight that you are now united in this way.

QUOTABLE QUOTES

And Ruth said, Entreat me not to leave thee,
or to return from following after thee: for whither thou
goest, I will go; and where thou lodgest, I will lodge: thy
people shall be my people, and thy God my God."
—*Bible. Ruth 1:8-16*

When brothers agree, no fortress is so strong
as their common life.
—*Antisthenes,* Greek philosopher

Cruel is the strife of brothers.
—*Aristotle,* Greek philosopher and educator

The family is the association established by nature
for the supply of men's everyday wants.
—*Aristotle,* Greek philosopher and scientist

The only rock I know that stays steady, the only
institution I know that works, is the family.
—*Lee Iacocca,* American businessman and author

Cherish your human connections:
your relationship with friends and family.
—*Barbara Pierce Bush*, American first lady and author

In my culture, there is no such thing as a single woman
alone with children. There is no such thing as
"alone" at all. There is the family.
—*Miriam Makeba*, South African singer and humanitarian

An ounce of blood is worth more
than a pound of friendship.
—*Anonymous*

The family the soul wants is a felt network of relationship, an evocation of a certain kind of interconnection
that grounds, roots, and nestles.
—*Thomas Moore*, Irish poet

Being a grown-up means assuming responsibility
for yourself, for your children, and—here's a big
curve—for your parents.
—*Wendy Wasserstein*, American playwright

Suggested Messages

- Welcome to the family of [Name]s. We all love our
  [Spouse's Name] so, and are delighted to see him so
  happy. We're delighted, too, that you have found each
  other. You two are so well matched in temperament,
  disposition, and even interests. And you're a wonderful
  golfer; what could be better in this family? We'd like to
  have you and [Spouse's Name] join us for a round of golf

and lunch on Saturday morning. This will give us all time to get better acquainted.

I'll call you Wednesday to see if this will work for you. I'm looking forward to lots of get-togethers in the future.

- We couldn't be happier. Our wonderful bachelor brother has chosen a bride. And such a wonderful partner he was fortunate enough to find. Welcome to the [Name] clan. We're delighted to have you as a sister-in-law, and we look forward to many happy times together.

- Welcome, sister-in-law. You have chosen wisely in a mate. [Name] is the most generous and kind person I know. I believe I'd say that even if he weren't my brother. You probably already know we're a demonstrative bunch without pretense or affectation. It can be a bit off-putting to the reserved, but we welcome you with open hearts, and we look forward to embracing you as one of this family.

- I'm sure there's not another family like ours. And I'm equally sure that we take some getting used to. But we are all thrilled to have you wearing our colors, and want you to know that we're here for you and [Name] for whatever you may need. Welcome to the family.

- [Name] and [Name], we're all over the moon here with happiness over the marriage of your daughter to our wonderful brother, [Name]. What a delightful couple they make. And adding you two to our family circle makes us all the happier. We're looking forward to seeing a lot more of you in the future. May we start with a summer picnic in our backyard on July 4? We'll do all the family games and it will give you the chance to meet everyone informally. (Hopefully, that won't be too much of a shock.)

- Yes, we [Name]s certainly have a few warts. But I believe you'll find us all accepting and loving. And we're the kind of family that puts family first. Now you're one of us. (That's not to imply that you have warts!) And we're very glad to have you. We believe you and [Name] will be very happy.

- Family makes life more beautiful, and that's the kind of resource we want to be for you and [Name]. I'm delighted to call you "Sis," and invite you to give me a call anytime with questions or just to chat. I probably know most of [Name]'s favorite family recipes, and nearly all his childhood diseases, since I'm the big sister. I'm looking forward to your future happiness as a couple, and to our new "sisterhood." Can we have lunch next week to get to know each other a bit better?

Message Etiquette

CREATING A STEP-RELATIVE RELATIONSHIP

Our high divorce rates and new social mores have produced legions of possible new relationships, but none more charged with emotional content than those between step-relatives. Often there are wounded loved ones who feel an interloper has usurped affection and focus that rightly belongs to her, or has intruded and taken a place she, alone, is entitled to inhabit. And the relationships are often further confused by feelings of anger, conflicted loyalties, and guilt many times over.

Whether it's between an adult and a child, or two adults, generous amounts of respect, care, and consideration must be carefully applied to produce harmony in a new family.

When children are at the center of new stepparent relation-ships, it's important that all the adults involved put aside any and all animosities and agree to always consider the children's wel-fare first. This means adults need to be the adults, and ensure that the children feel safe and secure, and free from parental conflicts.

Adopting the habit of writing reassuring messages to children can go a long way in establishing and maintaining their feelings of security.

Adult children, too, sometimes need such reassurances that their parents' love for them remains constant, and that they haven't been abandoned, or replaced, when the parent remarries. At the same time, adult children need to exercise their adult muscles and not hold their parents in a guilty embrace when a stepparent becomes part of the family picture.

Open acceptance and generosity are key in writing messages that welcome the new step-person(s) and promote family har-mony. You'll also want to close with a positive sentence or two about your hope for future happiness for everyone.

QUOTABLE QUOTES

Birds sing after a storm; why shouldn't people feel as free to delight in whatever sunlight remains to them?
—*Rose Fitzgerald Kennedy,* American president's mother and humanitarian

The long-term accommodation that protects marriage and other such relationships is . . . forgetfulness.
—*Alice Walker,* American author

> You hear a lot of dialogue on the death
> of the American family. Families aren't dying.
> They're merging into big conglomerates.
> —*Erma Bombeck,* American author

Suggested Messages
TO A YOUNG CHILD

- [Name], I know all the changes in your life have been hard, and sometimes confusing. I want you to understand that I also know I'm not your dad. You have a Dad, and that won't change. Your mom and I love each other, and we love you. We believe we can have a very special kind of family that cares for each of you, [Names of children], in a very special way.

- [Name], just so you know, [Name], Dad, and I are working very hard to be sure you'll still be doing all the things you did before [Name] and I got married. You'll be in the same Little League, in the same school, and even in your same bedroom. The thing that will be different is that you'll also be spending every other week at your dad's new house, and you can take [Dog's Name] with you. While you're there, your dad will take you to school and Little League, and for get-togethers with your friends. One other thing could be different: you might be having two birthday parties, instead of one. That wouldn't be so bad, would it?

- [Name], sometimes things have to change. Your dad and I did get a divorce, but we're not divorcing you. You are still our precious daughter—just like you always were, and just like you'll always be. We'll have to be moving and that will mean some changes, too. But our love for you won't change. We both love you very much.

- My marriage to [Name] doesn't change my love for you. You're still my Number One Son.

TO AN ADULT CHILD

- After you and [Name] left for college, I felt very lonely. I realized that you two were just keeping your end of our lifelong parent/child agreement: someday I'll grow up and leave you to lead my own life. I realized it, but I hated it. And I realized that I needed to create a whole new life for myself. I hated that, too. Then I met [Name], we fell in love, and are now planning on getting married. Yes, this changes some things, but it doesn't change my love for you and [Name]. I still love you both as much as ever, and am always here for you, regardless of what you need. And aren't you just a tiny bit relieved that all my happiness no longer depends on you?

- No, [Name], you aren't being replaced, usurped, or marginalized. My love for you remains constant. I believe if you search your heart you'll find the capacity to enlarge it enough to include [Name]. He'll be living in the "husband" room in my heart; there'll still be the same "daughter" room reserved completely and totally for you!

- [Name], I'm sure you wouldn't keep me from the love and companionship I now have with [Name] just to ensure that I love you as much as I always did. I'm not insisting that you love [Name], but I'm asking that we all decide to have the best relationship we can. Give it your best effort, will you?

Restoring a Relationship

When a connection with someone has been broken, there is a tear somewhere in your heart, and a longing to repair it. Being disconnected can rub the soul raw, and make the heart ache. When there has been a personal injury—perhaps more than at any other time—a special greeting card with your personal written message of contrition, or acceptance, will be a precious and valuable thing.

RECONNECTING

There's a great sense of rediscovery when you reconnect with someone. Maybe it's an old schoolmate you haven't heard from for years, a long-gone relative, or a former colleague. You, and she, may not even remember the last time you saw each other or communicated. But catching up is sure to be rewarding, and you may resolve not to suffer a future disconnect.

Message Etiquette

Your message should start with a warm greeting, and then include a sentence or two about past memories of your relationship, and perhaps a statement of regret that you have not been in contact, followed by a statement of your desire to have a future relationship. If there's another reason, too, for your message, you'll need to fold that in at the appropriate place.

QUOTABLE QUOTES

Let us not burden our remembrance with
A heaviness that's gone.
—*William Shakespeare,* English dramatist and poet

Anger kills both laughter and joy;
what greater foe is there than anger?
—*Tiruvalluvar,* Indian poet and sage

To regret deeply is to live afresh.
—*Henry David Thoreau,* American poet

Remorse is impotence; it will sin again.
Only repentance is strong; it can end everything.
—*Honoré de Balzac,* French author

He who forgives ends the quarrel.
—*Anonymous*

The time is always right to do what is right.
—*Martin Luther King, Jr.,* American clergyman and civil rights leader

Nature has given the opportunity of happiness to all,
knew they but how to use it.
—*Claudian,* Roman poet

I have loved badly, loved the great
Too soon, withdrawn my words too late;
And eaten in an echoing hall

Alone and from a chipped plate
The words that I withdrew too late.
—*Edna St. Vincent Millay,* American poet and playwright

Consider the rights of others before your own feelings,
and the feelings of others before your own rights.
—*John Wooden,* American basketball player and coach

Suggested Messages

- Why haven't I been in contact since [name a place or time]?

     I could cite a busy schedule, children, husband, and my job. But there would still be that niggling voice in the back of my head that always reminds me that I take the time to do what I really want to do.

     But I'm planning to come to the class reunion, and, of course, immediately thought of the Three Musketeers of [Name] High. I hope you're planning to attend, we can arrange a meeting, and catch up.

     I'm determined to do a better job in the future of keeping in touch. I promise.

- I know, of course, why we haven't been in touch. We both suffered from the breakup of [Name] and [Name], and felt strange—in the wake of all the animosity—about keeping in contact with each other. We were, after all, on opposite sides of that dispute.

     But I think you'll agree that it's a new season, the relationship of these former spouses has become civil, and there is no longer any reason for us to not repair our relationship.

     I've missed our daily discussions, and would like to

suggest we get together for lunch and a chat. We'll declare any mention of [Name] and [Name] off-limits, if you wish. I hope you'll agree. Please give me a call if this is something you'd like to do.

- I know why we stopped communicating. It was a silly, trivial thing I now realize, looking back with the wisdom of hindsight. I miss our old discussions and get-togethers, and would like to resume them if you're willing. I'll call you next week.

- Gosh, I miss you. We were once so close, if you remember. And how long has it been since we've talked or seen each other? I'm thinking about four years: that day in the grocery store when we ran into each other.

  Even though our kids have now graduated, and we no longer have the high school basketball games to connect us, let's do lunch and reconnect. If that sounds like a good idea, give me a call.

- Life is too short to be disconnected from one with whom I was once such a good friend. Let's reconnect and resume the magic. What do you say?

- Let's let the past be just that: the past. And let's resume the wonderful friendship we once had. Will you join me for lunch Wednesday, July 2, 12:30 P.M. at the Oxtail?

- We both have reason to feel alienated from the other, but I think we both feel, too, that life is too short to waste it cut off from each other. Let's get together and each listen with an open heart to the other's story about the breach in our relationship. OK? I suggest lunch at Sam's on the 14th at 12:30 P.M. Will that work for you?

APOLOGY

An apology is a peace offering you deliver to a person you offended. By offending someone, you created a debt you owe to that person. An apology repays it because it restores the dignity and self-respect she lost in the offense. An apology can also release the offended person to forgive you.

To work, the apology needs to be sincere. It also requires the best of human attributes: courage, honesty, humility, and generosity.

Message Etiquette

As in every social exchange, the apology needs to match the offense. When you have offended, start with a heartfelt desire to right the wrong. Then acknowledge the offense and take responsibility for it. If there are extenuating circumstances, explain them—but don't make excuses. Sincerely communicate your regret for committing the offense; make any reparations called for; and offer an olive branch as a show of your intended goodwill.

QUOTABLE QUOTES

Apology is only egotism wrong side out.
—*Oliver Wendell Holmes, Sr.,* American physician and author

A stiff apology is a second insult. . . . The injured party does not want to be compensated because he has been wronged; he wants to be healed because he has been hurt.
—*G. K. Chesterton,* English author

An apology has the power to generate forgiveness.
—*Aaron Lazare,* American physician, professor, and author

Suggested Messages

- I must apologize: my actions on Tuesday at the board meeting were boorish and rude. I now see why Grace did the accounting for the party the way she did, and it had nothing to do with not selling as many tickets as she'd promised. I'm emailing an apology to all the board members, but I wanted to also apologize to you personally and directly because I attacked your statement of explanation.

  I'm truly sorry, and I will be much more careful in studying the minutes and reports before the meeting in the future; and I'll ask any questions I have before the meeting, too.

- Guilty as charged! I feel terrible about dampening the spirit of your dinner party by appearing 40 minutes after everyone had begun the main course. I did call, of course, but knew you'd be unwired due to your hostess duties.

  Here's my story: I was rear-ended at State and Roosevelt, a very simple bumper crunch, but the policeman wasn't sympathetic to my pleas of needing to be somewhere else.

  I know that a vacant placesetting at such a gala event removes a bit of the shine and polish, and I'm so sorry. In fact, each one of these roses symbolizes a dozen "I'm so sorrys."

  But do let me say that the dessert and after-dinner party were delightful, [Name], as I'm sure the dinner was, too; and I so look forward to making <u>all</u> of your next social event.

- Please accept my apology. My remark about your new sofa was tactless. (My only defense is that I spend far too much time alone in my office writing, and have forgotten my social skills completely, especially my manners about critique.) Could you please find the grace to forgive me, to erase my comment from your memory, and to let me offer the following: Yes, I agree that adding the toss pillows in the colors of your wing chairs would create a more pleasing blend and balance to the room.

  Now, will you please come over on Sunday for dinner and critique my new living room furniture?

- Although Frisky shows no sincere remorse, I do want to apologize for his very bad behavior, and my lack of dog training skills. I'm so sorry he jumped on you this morning with his "I've just been on a walk" paws. I don't have to tell you that he failed the "down" portion of dog obedience training, and I, obviously, failed it, too.

  I'm enclosing a gift certificate for Diamond Cleaners to get your slacks cleaned, and I promise to work diligently on Frisky's guest manners. If you're brave enough, will you please come to tea next Tuesday at 4:00 P.M.? If I'm not completely confident about our canine's welcoming skills, I'll give him a time-out in the laundry room.

- I apologize for my behavior at your wedding reception. There's no excuse for being a sloppy drunken guest, and several people I've asked have confirmed that I was both loud and obnoxious. I'm mortified by my behavior, and can only offer the explanation that I'd been prescribed a new antidepressant by Dr. Leo Almo, and didn't read the potential side-effects about drinking alcohol as a warning not to drink a single glass of wine.

I know I can't make proper reparations for the spectacle I created, but I have certainly learned my lesson—if that's any consolation. I'm also sending an apology to your parents, and a thank-you note to your uncle for escorting me home.

I'd like to offer you my interior decorating services for an afternoon when you're ready as a token of my contrition. In addition, I'd also like to host a small dinner party for you, and [Name], and your parents when you return from your honeymoon.

FORGIVENESS

Electing to forgive someone who has offended you is a dynamic way of canceling the debt owed to you by her offense. Instead of accruing interest, or stewing in your anger and disappointment, you can elect to forgive the person instead. This process is usually aided by the apology, and it requires a change of mind and heart on your part. While it's true that your forgiveness is a gift you offer to the offender, it's also true that the act of forgiving pays big dividends to you, the offended person. It releases you from any anger you may still have, and even releases you from the desire to get revenge.

Message Etiquette

Start with the decision to forgive—that means giving up your anger and your desire for revenge. Once you've committed to forgiveness, begin the process of thinking of the person who offended you in a positive way. That's called reframing, and it requires that you empathize with the offender by imagining her reasons for the offense at the time and in the circumstances she committed it. Accept and absorb the pain of the offense without displacing it onto someone else. Then enjoy the sense of happiness and release from anger and distress that may now be yours in this new land you inhabit.

It's important to say here, too, that your forgiveness does not absolve the offender of the consequences of her offense. She is still obliged to make the proper (sometimes legal) reparations.

Nor does forgiving someone insinuate that you are obliged to continue to have a relationship with her. That is another decision you will have to make as a separate issue.

QUOTABLE QUOTES

To err is human, to forgive divine.
—*Alexander Pope,* English poet

The practice of forgiveness is our most important contribution to the healing of the world.
—*Marianne Williamson,* American author

Forgive us our debts, as we forgive our debtors.
—*Bible. Matthew 6:12*

Suggested Messages
- Yes, I do forgive you.
- Please know that I forgive you.
- I accept your apology, and I do forgive you.
- I refuse to let this come between us. I do forgive you.

- You most certainly do have my forgiveness. We are much too close for me to harbor ill will about this.
- I do know you are sorry, and I accept your apology. I forgive you.
- I've resolved my anger and desire for revenge. I forgive you.
- This goes against my first impulse, of course, but I've decided to take the path of forgiveness. And in doing so, I've found real peace.

PART SEVEN

Dates to Remember

*This record of dates will be very helpful to the book owner
who has resolved to make writing and connecting an
important part of her life. Be sure to include birth years,
wedding years, etc., so your record will become
a treasured resource.*

January

Name	Occasion	Date	Notations

February

Name	Occasion	Date	Notations

March

Name	Occasion	Date	Notations

April

Name	Occasion	Date	Notations

May

Name	Occasion	Date	Notations

June

Name	Occasion	Date	Notations

July

Name	Occasion	Date	Notations

August

Name	Occasion	Date	Notations

September

Name	Occasion	Date	Notations

October

Name	Occasion	Date	Notations

November

Name	Occasion	Date	Notations

December

Name	Occasion	Date	Notations

Notes

Notes